DIGGING UP
UNCLE EVANS

DIGGING UP UNCLE EVANS

HISTORY, GHOST TALES, & STORIES FROM OCRACOKE ISLAND

Philip Howard

Philip Howard

Black Squall Books
Ocracoke Island, North Carolina

Published by:
Black Squall Books
30 Lawton Lane
PO Box 701
Ocracoke, NC 27960

ISBN: 978-0-9816807-0-5

Library of Congress Control Number: 2008904373

Printed in the United States of America
1st printing

CONTENTS

In Memory of Lawton & Kunigunde Howard

OCRACOKE ISLAND

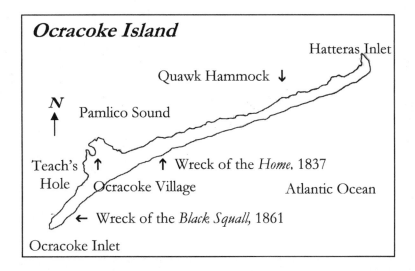

Ocracoke Island

Hatteras Inlet

Quawk Hammock ↓

N
↑

Pamlico Sound

Teach's ↑   ↑ Wreck of the *Home*, 1837
Hole   Ocracoke Village   Atlantic Ocean

← Wreck of the *Black Squall*, 1861

Ocracoke Inlet

O CRACOKE Island is approximately sixteen miles long, runs northeast to southwest, and lies about twenty-five miles across Pamlico Sound from the mainland of North Carolina. It is about two and a half miles wide in the vicinity of the village, and less than a quarter of a mile wide in other places. Mostly sandy banks, with the exception of the more stable village area, Ocracoke and surrounding islands of the Outer Banks have been the scene of nearly 1800 shipwrecks.

OCRACOKE VILLAGE

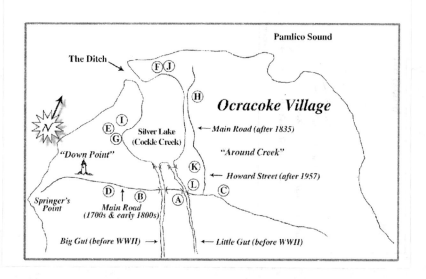

THE Ocracoke village map is not drawn to scale, and locations of houses and landmarks are approximate.

The general outline of the village area conforms to the shape of the island at the time this book was written. Erosion caused by hurricanes and other storms, and man-made intervention have altered the shape of the island over time. Houses and other structures noted on the map did not all exist in Ocracoke village at the same time. Some buildings have been moved. See text for details. The following structures were extant at the time of this writing: A, B, C, D, G, H, I, L.

Key:

)---(= Bridges over the Guts

A = Ocracoke Odd Fellows Lodge & Schoolhouse (1901-1916)/The Island Inn (Present)
B = James Henry Garrish House
C = Ocracoke Schoolhouse (1917-1971 & 1971-Present)
D = Bunia Foster House
E = Jacob Gaskill House
F = Willis Williams Tavern
G=John & Elizabeth McWilliams House (Fannie Pearl's Childhood Home)
H=Martha Ann Wahab House (Stanley Wahab's Childhood Home)
I = Captain William & Eliza Thomas House
J = Charlie & Sue Scarborough House
K = James & Zilphia Howard House
L = Homer & Aliph Howard House (the Author's Present Home)

PREFACE

S EVERAL years ago I began offering guided Ghost and History Walking Tours through the village of Ocracoke on Ocracoke Island, the southern-most island of the Outer Banks of North Carolina. The tours were the result of many years of earnestly collecting local stories and history. As a child I had listened to my father recount many of these alluring tales, and as a young adult I heard them repeated by the old-timers.

All too often I remembered only that "some old lady" had done so-and-so. Or that "years ago" this or that mysterious thing had happened. Or that there were "several bridges across the guts." But I didn't know who the old lady was, or how many years ago this curious event had transpired, or where exactly those bridges were.

I didn't know what the geography of the island was like before World War II. I didn't know anything about the earliest schoolhouses, or the first church build-ings, or the general stores in the 1800s.

In the 1950s, coastal schooners and other sailing vessels that had wrecked on our coast were little more than massive timbers protruding from the sand where I clambered and played.

Some of Ocracoke's most enchanting characters were vague memories, or images I had created in my mind.

But these characters were mostly my kinfolk. My ancestors were among those adventurous men who had captained some of the schooners whose skeletons lay on our beach. My great-grandfather was keeper of the Cedar Hammock Life Saving Station that was established at Hatteras Inlet in 1883, and it was he and his crew who had rescued many a hapless sailor.

My ancestors had sold the land for the schoolhouse and for the Methodist Church. They helped build both structures with their own hands. They encour-aged my grandparents to learn to read and write, and taught them to be strong and brave. But many of the old stories were quickly fading from memory.

Spurred on by the prospect of losing so much of this local tradition, I vowed to preserve as much as possible.

I spent countless hours visiting and talking with older residents, recording in my notebooks and on scraps of paper the many intriguing stories and local histories that were increasingly in danger of being forgotten.

In time I had collected so many tales that I was asked to share some of them on Wednesday evenings in the summer months at Deepwater Theater's popular *Ocrafolk Opry*.

Also, I was encouraged to offer a walking tour for summer visitors. The result was two distinct tours, one on the south side of Silver Lake (the "Down Point" tour), the other on the north side of Silver Lake (the "Around Creek" tour).

Not surprisingly, many of the folks who took my tours (and that included a number of local residents) insisted that I put the tales down in book form. The order of the stories in this volume, *Digging up Uncle Evans*, generally follows the order of the stories on the Down Point walking tour.

The tour begins on historic Howard Street, across from the many small family cemeteries there. It follows the School Road, and then continues past the Island Inn on the way to the lighthouse. From there it turns back toward Silver Lake, then follows the road around the harbor and back to Lawton Lane, and thence to the beginning on Howard Street.

A companion volume is scheduled for publication in the future. It will include tales from the other walking tour.

The remainder of the stories I have collected will fill several more volumes.

In the meanwhile, sit back, prop up your feet, relax, and enjoy some of our singular island tales.

Philip Howard
Ocracoke Island
www.blacksquallbooks.com
Spring, 2008

A note about style: Eighteenth and nineteenth century letters and documents that are included in this book sometimes contain elements that are unfamiliar to modern readers. Nevertheless, in the following pages I have retained the original grammar and spelling, although I have sometimes divided longer excerpts into paragraphs for ease of reading.

A Perplexing Dream

IT is 1959. Midnight is approaching and I am standing beside the venerable and lonely graves on Howard Street, a narrow sandy lane in Ocracoke village. Silence has descended upon the graveyards, covering the dead like a heavy blanket. Menacing storm clouds scud across the heavens threatening to obscure the full moon which hangs heavy in the sky.

Howard Street

I am fifteen years old and my trembling hands rest on an ancient wooden fence. Several pickets are broken, others are missing. Most are covered with pale mosses and lichens. A gate hangs forlornly from one rusty hinge. The scent of decay floats in the air. I am peering intently into the semi-darkness, into my own family graveyard on this deserted lane.

Live oaks and cedars reach above my head, forming a dark tunnel. The graveyards are overgrown with briars and grapevines and weeds. They have been so for centuries. But I blink my eyes…and curiously the scene changes.

The marble and granite markers are now stretched out on the trackless bald beach. For miles there is nothing but tombstones and tidal flats…and a few low dunes crowned with sea oats bending under the assault of the west wind. Beyond is the angry, churning Atlantic Ocean. I am gazing not only into a dream world, but also into the past, into the "time of the blowing sand."

As I watch, the wind sweeps away the sand in front of a timeworn marble tombstone. Slowly an unfamiliar object emerges from the ground. It is a skull. The sand swirls and spirals upwards, carried away by the howling wind. More and more of the skeleton lies exposed. The rib cage, the pelvis, the arms, the legs. The skull turns slowly and deliberately in my direction. Its vacant, hollow eye sockets seem to lock me in a penetrating gaze.

Terrified, I watch as the bones rise slowly from the grave and move in my direction. The fence has disappeared. Nothing but sandy soil separates me from this dreaded creature.

Suddenly the skeleton raises its arms and lunges toward me. I step backwards just in time to evade its grasp. Now I am retreating quickly.

It is then that I notice an especially peculiar detail. The skeleton has no fingertips. The other bones are there, but the ends of the skeleton's fingers are missing. Somehow this makes the horror even more terrifying. I turn and run away. The skeleton chases. I know it is after me, close on my heels. Faster and faster I run, through silent burying grounds, across sand flats, then past abandoned, weathered old houses with windows missing and doors ajar, farther onto the bald beach.

And then I disappear, engulfed by a blinding sandstorm.

I awake…sweating, my heart racing. It takes me an hour or more to return to sleep.

I have the dream not once, not twice, but often. Always the same. Always that skeleton rising from the swirling sand and chasing me with upraised arms, always missing the tips of its fingers.

In a way familiar to anyone who has ever had a nightmare, my dream of the skeleton rising from the grave was a strange mixture of images. I was standing by the graveyards on historic Howard Street. Suddenly the cemeteries and I were transformed, and I was standing alone on the edge of the bald beach at the time of the blowing sand, an era in Ocracoke's history of dramatic environmental and social change.

Ocracoke Island has always been a dynamic, evolving place. Little was understood about the constantly changing Outer Banks in 1719 when a tract of land containing 2,110 acres was conveyed by the Lords Proprietors to John Lovick. This grant was for land "[b]eginning at Hatteras Inlet and running to Occacok Inlet," what we today would call Ocracoke Island.

In 1721 Lovick sold the island to Charles Eden, Governor of North Carolina, but somehow got it back again after Eden's death in 1722. Lovick then sold Ocracoke to Richard Sanderson who deeded one half of the island to the privateer Roger Kenyon in 1723. By some now long-forgotten transaction, Sanderson obtained full ownership of Ocracoke again, before his death in 1733. At that time "Ye Island of Ocreecock, with all the stock of horses, sheep, cattle and hoggs" was bequeathed to his son, Richard Sanderson.

There is no evidence that John Lovick, Governor Eden, Roger Kenyon or either of the Sandersons ever made their homes on the island.

On July 13, 1759 Richard Sanderson, Jr. sold his 2,110 acres to William Howard, Sr. for £105.

It is difficult to determine exactly what was granted and sold in this early period of Ocracoke's history. Violent storms, accompanied by strong winds and rushing tides are constantly shaping and reshaping these fragile barrier islands. The only Outer Banks inlet that has been continuously open since Europeans began keeping records is Ocracoke Inlet.

Present-day Hatteras Inlet was opened by a fierce storm in 1846. Prior to that time other inlets existed, and the north end of what is now Ocracoke Island and the south end of Hatteras Island were connected, creating an intermediate island.

Today there are seven tidal creeks on Ocracoke Island that intersect North Carolina Highway 12. From north to south they are Try Yard Creek, Parker's Creek, Quawk's Point Creek, Molasses Creek, Old Hammock Creek, Shad Hole Creek (now mostly dried up), and Island Creek.

Although these creeks are open to Pamlico Sound they do not extend all the way to the Atlantic Ocean. They are undoubtedly remnants of previous inlets.

In 1759 Ocracoke Island was approximately half of its present length (today it is about sixteen miles long). At that time a true inlet must have existed in the area where one of the northernmost creeks flows today.

Present day Ocracoke Island includes about 5,535 acres. If we exclude the village of Ocracoke (which consists of about 775 acres) we are left with 4,760 acres of "sandy banks." Half of this is 2,380 acres, very close to the area recorded in the earliest deeds.

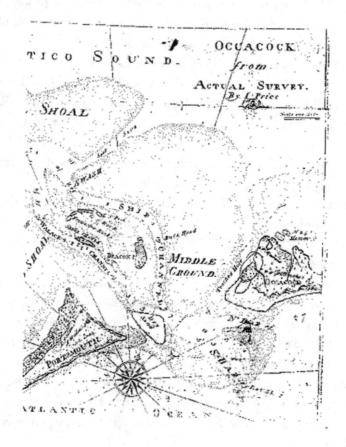

Jonathan Price Map, 1795

In 1795 Jonathan Price produced a detailed map of Ocracoke Inlet, accompanied by a description of the area. Referring to the village and its surroundings, Price wrote, "Occacock was heretofore, and still retains the name of, an island. It is now a peninsula; a heap of sand having gradually filled up the space which divided it from the bank. It continues to have its former appearance from the sea; the green trees, that cover it, strikingly distinguishing it from the sandy bank to which it has been joined. Its length is three miles, and its breadth two and one half. Small live oak and cedar grow abundantly over it, and it contains several swamps and rich marshes, which might be cultivated to great advantage; but its inhabitants, depending on another element for their support, suffer the earth to remain in its natural state. They are all pilots; and their number of head of families is about thirty."

This description presents some confusion for the modern reader. Ocracoke (historically spelled many different ways, including Occacok, Ocreecock, and Occacock) seems to refer sometimes to the sandy banks and at other times to a separate island where Ocracoke village is located today. Clearly Price uses Occacock to mean the village area. In contrast, earlier deeds for Occacok and Ocreecock probably referred only to the sandy banks.

This naturally leads to speculation that William Howard, last colonial owner of Ocracoke, and the first owner to live on the island, may have already been living in the nascent village when he purchased an additional 2,110 acres of the sandy banks in 1759.

In 1715 the North Carolina Colonial Assembly passed an act for "settling and maintaining Pilots at…Ocacock Inlett." Piracy was ascendant at that time, and legislators recognized that the remote and unprotected outer islands were vulnerable to the depredations of unsavory characters. As late as 1753 the Colonial Assembly was still mentioning "Insults from Pirates and other rude People" as one of the justifications for appropriating funds to build a fortification on nearby Portsmouth Island.

In 1718 Blackbeard and other buccaneers were so effectively terrorizing the coast of North Carolina that few colonists were willing to risk life and property to move to Ocracoke. It was not until sometime in the 1730s that the first pilots made permanent settlements on the island.

William Howard was likely one of these first pilots. Research suggests that he was born about 1686 and was almost certainly the same William Howard who served as Blackbeard's quartermaster in 1717 and 1718. Captured in the summer of 1718, Howard was tried and sentenced to death in Williamsburg, Virginia. Since he was confined to jail in November of 1718 when Blackbeard was overtaken and killed near Ocracoke Inlet, William Howard was spared death in Blackbeard's final battle. Howard's life was saved again when the king's "Act of

Grace" arrived in the colonies the day before his execution in December. After his release he may have spent time in both Maryland and North Carolina, but there is nothing to suggest that he ever returned to piracy.

In his seventies when he purchased land from Richard Sanderson, William Howard seems by then to have been well established on Ocracoke. It is difficult to believe that at that age he suddenly moved from the mainland, along with his entire family, to this remote barrier island. More likely, he had settled on the island as a younger man, had accumulated extra funds, and finally had the opportunity to increase his holdings.

An undated newspaper article written by Ocracoke native Amasa Fulcher (1876—1946) states that the conveyance of 2,110 acres of land lying between Hatteras and Ocracoke Inlets ("Ye Island of Ocreecock") "leads us to believe that at this time [the early 1700s] there was an Inlet just north of the neighborhood where is now located what we call the Plains [the area from the edge of the village to the National Park Service Campground]."

Fulcher goes on to say that "[o]lder people of Ocracoke used to refer to this section as Nigh Inlet, and…Hatteras Inlet…was located south of the Hatteras Inlet Coast Guard station…."

According to older island residents, their parents and grandparents would sometimes remark that very many years ago grape vines and other vegetation grew so thick that they formed sturdy mats in the trees that children routinely played in. Several reports have survived that a thick mat of vines and briars originating in the trees near the graveyards on Howard Street was so extensive that it was common for young boys to climb to the top and crawl all the way to the sea.

Islanders of today often wonder how that could be. The Atlantic Ocean is almost three quarters of a mile from the southeastern end of present-day Howard Street. Furthermore, in the mid-twentieth century fully half of that distance, the area of the island that extended from the edge of the village (where Old Beach Road is located today) to the ocean, was a wide tidal flat virtually devoid of vegetation.

How could it be that grapevines at one time extended to the very edge of the sea?

In 1795 Jonathan Price wrote of the "small live oak and cedar" which "grow abundantly over [the village]." The vegetation in the area of the village was at that time, and still is, noticeably different from the natural vegetation on the "banks." In contrast to the barren tidal flats and occasional dunes covered by sea oats and other highly salt tolerant plants and grasses, the "live oak[s] and cedar[s]" and the "swamps and rich marshes" of the village suggest a different geologic formation.

The "sea" must have meant, not the Atlantic Ocean, but a channel of water separating Ocracoke village from the sandy banks. At the end of the eighteenth century, when just a handful of hearty souls were calling Ocracoke home, the village area, once a separate island, seems to have become connected to the banks by a buildup of sand, and Price described it as a peninsula.

But that area was inherently unstable and over the next century and a half the waterway that had once separated Ocracoke village from the banks continued to advance and retreat, the buildup of sand periodically reverting to a swash or channel between the banks and the village.

The dynamic nature of the North Carolina Outer Banks is apparent in the changing shape of Ocracoke Island. As late as the 1970s and early 1980s the area between the edge of the village and the airstrip (including North Carolina Highway 12) would often be covered with salt water during storms and exceptionally high tides.

Only in the 1980s did engineers stop the process by building up the roadbed of NC Highway 12, limiting vehicle traffic to one raised corridor to the South Point, and encouraging the introduction of grasses, shrubs, and trees in the low lying areas nearby.

For many years, from the early eighteenth century until the mid-twentieth century, grazing livestock would have periodically been able to wander across tidal flats, or even a shallow swash, from the sandy banks into Ocracoke village, and back again.

Unfortunately, the introduced livestock population increased rapidly, and much of the island's natural vegetation was soon eradicated due to overgrazing. Sheep were especially destructive, but goats, cattle, and horses contributed to the problem as well. In addition, demand for lumber, especially southern live oak for shipbuilding, hastened denuding of the island landscape.

During the eighteenth century the British Navy engaged in a practice called "live oaking." Hardwoods were aggressively harvested in the colonies for ships. In particular, shipbuilders sought live oaks. The felled logs were tied together in bundles and carried offshore where they were set adrift in the Gulf Stream. From there they would float across the Atlantic. A goodly number of the bundles actually arrived on the west coast of England where the British Navy gathered them and turned them into ship timbers.

Ocracoke Islanders have passed down stories of early shipbuilders and their agents who walked from house to house examining the many live oaks that grew in the village. When they spotted a tree that was especially large, or that grew in such a way as to produce one or more natural "knees," an important component of tall ships and schooners, they would approach the homeowner and offer an enticing sum to purchase the tree.

In this way a number of Ocracoke's majestic old-growth live oaks were harvested in the 1700s and the early- to mid-1800s. This, coupled with over-grazing, had disastrous results. By the end of the nineteenth century so much of the island had been stripped of its vegetation that islanders began referring to this period as the time of the blowing sand.

Homeowners who had built on the eastern edge of Ocracoke village, an area that had originally been covered by trees, bushes, and thick undergrowth, slowly found themselves confronted with a desert-like landscape. Villagers would wake in the morning to find sand piled around their houses, often so deep that it was impossible to open the doors. It drifted through cracks in the walls and passed through openings around windows and doors. Eventually fine sand covered some houses up to the windowsills.

Much of the original wide mat of grape vines was gone. Now there was a mile or more of bald beach extending from the edge of the village all the way to the Atlantic Ocean.

Many of Ocracoke's Bragg family, whose ancestors had called Ocracoke home since the late 1700s, found their land overtaken with the blowing sand. Their property included a wide swath from the present-day School Road to beyond Cedar Road, where the East Carolina Bank sits today. As the bald beach advanced, the Braggs gradually abandoned their homes and moved closer to Cockle Creek (Silver Lake). Sometimes they dismantled their houses and rebuilt them at a safer distance from the bare beach. At other times they would set a house down on sturdy logs, hook a team of horses to it, and roll the house to a new location. Often they simply allowed nature to claim their homes.

Particularly distressing during this time was the state of the Bragg family cemeteries. Strong, unrelenting winds blew steadily over their graves, slowly uncovering them. Residents periodically discovered caskets protruding from the blowing sand. At older gravesites the caskets had deteriorated, and skulls and other bones were sometimes exposed. Islanders recall hearing stories about a woman's body that was swept clean of its sandy covering. Some even remember that for a time her matted red hair could be seen fluttering wildly in the frigid winter wind.

Eventually the Bragg family contacted some of the Howards and asked for land to bury their dead. Close examination of the graveyards on Howard Street today reveals more than a half dozen Bragg tombstones.

Several years ago I was sitting in the parlor of my cousin's 90 year old house on Howard Street, a pile of genealogical papers spread out on her card table. Talk turned to relatives long dead and old family stories. One thing led to another, and directly we were discussing the graveyards on Howard Street...and the distant ancestors buried there.

She reminded me of a particularly interesting story about the burial of my Uncle Evans in 1923, a story in which my immediate family played a significant role. I had heard it many times, but somehow I had never made the obvious connection between this story and my distressing dream of the skeleton without its finger bones...until that moment.

But the conclusion of this story is best saved until the end of the book, or, better yet, the end of the day...best saved until that timeless period between the half-light of a dying day and the murky darkness of the witching hour.

So please, light your oil lamp, settle down in a comfortable chair, turn the page, and enjoy these authentic tales, maritime history, and stories from Ocracoke Island.

A BRIEF HISTORY OF OCRACOKE ISLAND

O CRACOKE Island! The name itself suggests history, enchantment, even magic. The earliest recorded names for the island (Wococon, Wokokon, Wococock) reflect the island's Native American heritage. Ocracoke's first residents were members of the pre-Columbian Wocon tribe who lived up the Neuse River. Whether these Algonquian-speaking natives ever established year-round settlements on the island, or simply visited Ocracoke seasonally to hunt, fish, and gather shellfish, no one knows.

Recent evidence on nearby Hatteras Island indicates that "Croatoan" (the island on John White's map of 1585 which includes the southern part of present-day Hatteras Island and portions of Ocracoke Island) was home to a tribe of Native Americans at the time of European colonization.

As of this writing at least eight Native American archeological sites have been located on Hatteras Island. One excavation site in the modern village of Buxton is believed to be the capital of the Croatan society. The Croatans were the Algonquian-speaking natives who greeted the first English settlers to the area in 1584—1587.

Someday we might discover evidence of a Wocon village on Ocracoke Island. In the meanwhile we can only speculate that these people made the twenty-five mile journey across Pamlico Sound only periodically, mainly to feast on the abundant seafood in these waters.

Some say that the Wocon Indians eventually intermingled with the nearby Waccamaw tribe and were completely assimilated. Or perhaps some of them intermarried with Ocracoke's early settlers. There is an old saying on Ocracoke, "He's been around as long as old Tannabogus." No one alive knows who old Tannabogus was, or even if this was a man or a woman. But legend suggests that Tannabogus was a Native American who died at an advanced age on the island more than two hundred years ago.

Eventually the "W" was dropped from Wococon, vowels and consonants were changed and added, and spellings such as "Okok" and "Ocrcok" evolved into the present-day "Ocracoke."

In spite of the legend that has Blackbeard crying out "Oh Crow Cock" on that fateful morning of November 22, 1718, when he engaged Lt. Robert Maynard in his final naval battle, the name "Ocracoke," as noted above, is undoubtedly of much earlier Native American origin.

Roger Payne, in his book, *Place Names of the Outer Banks*, speculates that Wococon could even be a tortured Anglicization of the Algonquian word "waxi-hikami" which means "enclosed place, fort, or stockade."

David Stick, in his book, *Roanoke Island, the Beginnings of English America*, has another explanation. When Walter Raleigh's expedition set foot on Ocracoke in 1584, he suggests, they asked the natives they encountered what the name of their country was. In reply they answered "Wingandacon," which became "Wococon." In truth, Stick tells us, the actual reply was "You wear good clothes."

Over the years I have seen dozens of different spellings for the present-day Ocracoke Island. Curious, I compiled a list of all the variations I could document. Ultimately I discovered more than fifty distinct names and/or spellings for Ocracoke.

The chart at the end of this chapter lists eighteen different spellings (highlighted in gray), as well as a number of duplicates, from a series of early maps and other documents. Other spellings are listed after the chart. The earliest record of the current "Ocracoke" occurs on a map drawn by A. D. Bache dated 1852.

Ocracoke played a part in the early English colonization of the New World when, in June of 1585, one fleet of Sir Walter Raleigh's expedition, in attempting to reach Roanoke Island, landed at Ocracoke.

According to Richard Hakluyt's history of the Raleigh expeditions, "…a fleet of seven vessels…under the command of Sir Richard Grenville…passed the Cape Feare on June 23rd and days later came to anchor at Wokokon southwest of Cape Hatterask." The *Tiger*, Sir Richard Grenville's flagship, ran aground in Ocracoke Inlet on June 29, 1585.

Sonny Williamson, in his *Shipwrecks of Ocracoke Island*, reports that after reaching Wococon Inlet the expedition entered Pamlico Sound with smaller vessels, all of which ran aground but were re-floated without damage. The next day they brought the *Tiger* inside and she became stranded in a "pounding surf" for two hours.

After being re-floated, the *Tiger* was beached, inspected, repaired, and launched again. Although her cargo had been completely soaked in salt water, the *Tiger* was sound and she continued on her journey.

Little of note happened at Ocracoke for more than one hundred and twenty-five years. Meanwhile, after the restoration of the British monarchy in 1660 following the overthrow of Oliver Cromwell's puritanical rule, the newly crowned king, Charles II, revoked his father's earlier grant of Carolina to Sir Robert Heath. As a reward for faithful support, the king then granted the colony of "Carolana" (including Ocracoke Island) to eight Lords Proprietors in 1663.

Pirates contributed particularly colorful chapters to the island's history in the early eighteenth century. Captain Edward Teach, a fearless and daring brigand of the seas, counted Ocracoke among his favorite anchorages, and was a close personal friend of North Carolina's colonial governor, and one-time owner of Ocracoke Island, Charles Eden.

After eighteen months of plunder and pillage along the eastern seaboard, Teach, best known to history simply as Blackbeard, was killed in a fierce naval battle at Ocracoke Inlet on November 22, 1718.

Buccaneers continued to use the island as a temporary campsite even after the infamous pirate's demise, but the "golden age" of piracy was over.

The history of individual European ownership of Ocracoke Island begins on November 11, 1719 when John Lovick, a Welsh Quaker, Secretary of the Colony of North Carolina, and a Deputy of the Lords Proprietors, was granted the island of "Ocacock," containing 2,110 acres.

Because larger vessels were unable to navigate the shallow Pamlico Sound, Ocracoke Island soon became a settlement for maritime pilots who transported sought-after goods to ports on the North Carolina mainland.

On July 30, 1759 William Howard, of the Province of North Carolina, bought Ocracoke Island for £105. Many of his descendants continue to live on the island to this day.

Over the next two hundred years Ocracoke prospered and grew. Located near the southern end of the island, and nestled around one of the most beautiful natural harbors in the new country, Ocracoke village attracted sailors, pilots, and commercial fishermen. Eventually, as sturdier homes were built and more families were raised on this remote ribbon of sand, stores, churches, and schools were established. By the turn of the twenty-first century the year-round population had grown to about 750.

Throughout its history Ocracoke and its people have been witnesses to a number of important events. Ocracoke Inlet, with its deep and navigable channel, was a strategic point of entry into Pamlico Sound, and ultimately to mainland North Carolina during both the Revolutionary and Civil Wars. During the War Between the States local residents served proudly in both the Union and Confederate armies. Fort Ocracoke, on nearby Beacon Island, was the scene of a naval attack in 1861. The fortress was abandoned during that time, and later destroyed. Recently, marine archaeologists have uncovered numerous artifacts in the vicinity.

World War II saw the construction of a naval base on Silver Lake Harbor and the erection of the United States' first radar tower near the beach on what is now known as Loop Shack Hill. The war was closer to our shores than many Americans realized. Throughout the conflict local residents reported seeing numerous ships burning offshore as the result of aggressive U-boat activity.

The British Cemetery, next to the historic George Howard family graveyard, is the final resting place of four sailors from *HMT Bedfordshire* which was torpedoed on May 11, 1942.

HMT Bedfordshire

Island residents discovered their bodies on the beach shortly after the tragedy and arranged for fitting burials under the shade of several large live oaks. Today the graves are under the care of the British War Graves Commission, the U.S.

Coast Guard, and the Graveyard of the Atlantic Museum. Every spring, a memorial service is held to honor these and other brave sailors who served in WWII.

British Cemetery

Ocracoke residents have survived not only world political unrest, but hurricanes and shipwrecks as well. In the 1800s many islanders were owners, captains, or sailors on schooners that plied waters along the eastern seaboard. Over the years more than 1800 vessels have met their fate in the waters around nearby Diamond Shoals. Many older homes in the Ocracoke historic district were built with lumber salvaged from ships that wrecked in storm-tossed seas. Not a few local residents are direct descendants of the brave men who served in the U.S. Life Saving Service. Their heroic deeds during many a daring rescue constitute a noble legacy that has been passed on to the younger generations.

Major hurricanes in 1899, 1933, and 1944, as well as more recent storms, have pummeled the island with high winds and rising water. Although native islanders all have stories of exciting encounters with ferocious storms, very little property damage has resulted, and no islander has ever lost a life in a hurricane.

Seven miles northeast of the village the National Park Service cares for the descendants of a once-wild herd of ponies. Some believe the original ponies were brought to the island by the earliest settlers. Others think they swam ashore from ships that wrecked on nearby sand bars. For years Ocracoke hosted an annual Independence Day pony penning. In the mid-1950s Captain Marvin Howard organized the only mounted Boy Scout troop in the country.

Ocracoke Lighthouse

Probably Ocracoke's best loved structure is the picturesque white lighthouse. Built in 1823, this beacon is one of the oldest still in active service in the United States. The steady beam can be seen up to 14 miles out to sea and serves as the most recognized symbol of the community of Ocracoke.

Due to years of cultural isolation many native Ocracokers still speak a distinctive brogue and continue to celebrate their unique island heritage.

Many readers of this book will have visited Ocracoke Island at least once. Others will surely be longtime friends of the island. I suspect that not a few will be residents or natives. I hope everyone finds in these stories a glimpse into an island and a community that I love dearly. Ocracoke is a unique outpost that boasts a rich history and a colorful past. If I have helped preserve even a tiny part of that heritage in this book I will be richly rewarded.

Date	Name	Document	Author
1585	Wococon	map	John White
1585	Wokokon	map	John White
1590	Wokokon	map	White—DeBry
1606	Wococon	map	Mercator-Hondius
1657	Wococock	map	Nicholaus Comberford
1665	Wococock	survey	T. Woodward
1665	Wococon	survey	T. Woodward
1672	Okok	map	Ogilby
1675	Okok	map	John Speed
1682	Wosoton	map	Joel Gascoyne & Robert Greene
1689	Wossoton	map	John Thorton & Will Fisher
1706	Wocoton	map	Johannes Loots
1709	Ocacok	map	John Lawson
1715	Occacock	act of the assembly	NC Assembly
1715	Occacoke	map	Henry Mouzon
1717	Occeh	letter	Gov. Spotswood
1718	Occocock	Historical account	annonymous
1732	Ocacock	Document/letter	Capt. Burrington
1733	Ocacock	map	Edward Moseley
1733	Ocreecock	deed	Richard Sanderson
1733	Oakerccok	map	James Wimble
1738	Okerccok	map	James Wimble
1770	Occacock	map	John Collet
1775	Occacoke	map	Henry Mouzon
1795	Occacock	map/description	Jonathan Price
1808	Occacock	map	Price—John Strother
1821	Ocracock	map	Leut. Strong
1833	Ocracock	map	Mac Rae—Brazier

1834	Occacock	map	H.S. Tanner
1852	Ocracoke	map	A.D. Bache
1861	Occacock	map	J.H. Colton
1861	Ocracoke	map	Bachman

In addition to the spellings listed above, I have located the following 33 variations, mentioned in an assortment of books and pamphlets, although no original sources were cited: Oa Cock, Oacock, Oakacock, Oakocock, Ocacoc, Ocacok, Occacode, Occacoe, Occek, Ocock, Ococock, Ocraacocke, Ocracook, Ocrecock, Ocrecok, Oecceh, Okercock, Okcrecock, Okerecock, Okerecok, Onoconon, Sequotan, Vokoton, Wakokon, Woccock, Woccocon, Woccon, Woccocock, Wococan, Wocoken, Wocotan, Wosotan, Woston

These do not include other names by which Ocracoke was sometimes known, such as Pilot Town, Port Bath, Port Grenvil, and Gordon's Ile. One of the more enduring early spellings was "Occacock."

MRS. GODFREY'S GHOST

I didn't recognize the woman right away, although she had been on my Ghost and History Tour the summer before. She and almost two dozen other people were with me on that July evening. We stopped at the Island Inn, as we always do.

This is the building that had originally been built as Ocracoke's Odd Fellows Lodge and Schoolhouse.

Island Inn Stairway

The Island Inn, now more than one hundred years old, is host to one of the island's most active ghosts, and I was sharing details. Standing in the parking lot just after dusk I recounted the basic history of the structure and then told the gruesome tale of Mrs. Godfrey's murder.

Most people recoil at the telling.

The story is not complete without sharing the sightings and strange happenings experienced by employees and guests alike.

I had not quite finished my tale when the woman felt compelled to tell her story. Some years before, she had rented a room at the Inn. After a day of exploring the island she returned to the hotel lobby and climbed the antique stairway to her second floor accommodations.

At the entrance to her room she retrieved the key from her purse and slowly opened the door. It was quiet inside. A delicate breeze wafted through the open window and gently rustled the lace curtains. She was exhausted. The old iron bed, piled high with soft pillows and a cozy quilt beckoned to her. But she could not sleep yet. Her mind raced with images of sailors, pirates, and simple island folks who had called Ocracoke home for generations. What was it like, she wondered, to live here, so far from conventional civilization? Who had built this fine hotel, and what stories did it hold?

Finally, too tired to think any more, she prepared for bed, and turned in about an hour before midnight. Several hours later, aroused from a deep sleep, she had the distinct sensation that someone was holding on to her big toe. She forced herself awake, afraid at first to open her eyes, fearful of what she might see.

With trepidation she lifted her head slowly and opened her eyes. Instantly the sensation vanished. No one was standing at the foot of her bed, and no hand grasped her toe. The curtains were still.

Convinced it had merely been a disquieting dream, she drifted back to sleep, only to be awakened a second time with the identical sensation. Again, no person, no figure, presented itself. And the pressure on her toe disappeared the moment she opened her eyes.

After the third encounter with whatever was holding on to her toe the woman propped herself on her pillows and determined to stay awake until daybreak. In the morning she requested to be moved to one of the newer rooms in the building on the other side of the street.

After hearing the stories of Mrs. Godfrey, she said, she now knew who had been tormenting her that night.

The center section of what is now the Island Inn was constructed several hundred feet closer to Cockle Creek than where it sits today. It was built by one of the island's most respected carpenters, Mr. Charlie Scarborough, in 1901.

The ground floor of the Lodge housed the island's first community school. In 1917 students moved to a new schoolhouse that was built near Howard Street. Sometime around 1920, following the death of Michael Lawrence Piland, a Gates County native who many believe introduced the Independent Order of Odd Fellows to Ocracoke, the fraternal organization was disbanded. The Lodge was sold and converted to a private residence. A few years later the building was moved to protect it from periodically rising storm tides.

Mr. Charlie's grandson, Alton, tells how the new owner, Ben O'Neal, asked Charlie, after church one Sunday morning, to supervise the move. Charlie allowed as how it would take him a week to make preparations. During that time Charlie had some tall, straight trees cut down and trimmed to use as rollers. The building was jacked up and a team of horses readied.

On the following Sunday after services Charlie announced that he would move the Lodge the next day and called for all the able-bodied men to be there at sunup. He was offering wages of thirty-five cents per day as enticement.

As the men gathered, one among them was known to all as a slacker, a grumbler, and an all-around slouch. The other workers wondered aloud if he was to be paid the same thirty-five cents as they were.

Ben O'Neal Home, ca. 1925

Charlie got wind of the discontent and devised a novel plan. He walked to an old stump lying nearby and rolled it over toward the side of the building. "Sit right down here," Charlie admonished the ne'er-do-well. "I'm payin' you the same thirty-five cents I'm payin' everyone else. But your job is to gripe and complain. Tell everyone within earshot how the pay is too little, how the work is too hard, how we're doin' everything the wrong way, how it's too hot, and that there's the greatest bunch of skeeters here you've ever seen."

"And the rest of you," Charlie exhorted, "are to keep your mouths shut and work! There's no need for fussin' and moanin' from any of you now. That's all to be done right from this here stump…and we'll be finished by dinnertime!"

And they were.

In 1940 the building was sold again, this time to Robert Stanley Wahab, native islander and early entrepreneur. Immediately the first floor was converted into a coffee shop with soda fountain and ice cream bar. Rooms upstairs became a boarding house. Later, during the war, the second floor was converted again, this time to an exclusive club for Navy Officers. It was dubbed the "Crow's Nest."

Robert Stanley Wahab

After the war a number of improvements and additions were made to the building. A sizeable northeast wing was added in the 1950s that included a dining hall and more guest quarters. Later on several former Navy barracks were moved and attached to the southwest side of the building. Newly christened the Silver Lake Inn, the former Lodge was now a modern hotel. In addition to guest rooms and a dining facility, the Inn also included a dance hall.

Local musicians gathered there on Saturday nights to play for the traditional Ocracoke square dances. After suppers of flounder, Irish potatoes, collards, and corn bread, young men and women walked barefoot through sandy lanes to meet at the Lodge. Banjoes, guitars, fiddles, and metal triangles rang out with fast-paced tunes as the caller led dancers through figures such as the Ocean Wave, Birdie in the Cage, and Dive for the Oyster, Dig for the Clam. Homemade meal wine flowed freely from jugs stashed away under nearby trees, and many a church-going parent worried about growing evil influences. Nevertheless, the Silver Lake Inn had become a prominent landmark and social center for residents and visitors alike.

The Inn was sold in the 1960s and the name changed to the Island Inn. There is no longer a dance hall associated with the Inn, but the present owners continue to serve the traveling public with comfortable rooms, private baths, and even a swimming pool.

As an added benefit, present day guests at the Island Inn, especially those who occupy rooms on the upper floors of the older section of the building, are sometimes confronted by the ghost of Mrs. Godfrey, a former resident.

During the war Stanley Wahab hired a couple from the mainland to act as managers for his growing hotel. They took an apartment in the hotel. Although capable employees, they soon became well known on the island for their domestic squabbles. Islanders remember them "fighting like cats and dogs." It became an embarrassment to many Ocracokers, who seldom allowed their private lives to be displayed so publicly.

In those days all of the roads on Ocracoke were primitive sandy lanes. Ferry service to Hatteras and eastern North Carolina was nothing more than a vague dream. Ocracoke's primary link to the mainland was by mail boat. The forty-two foot *Aleta* could carry several dozen passengers—a few in her cabin, others on benches under a protective canvas awning, and more on wooden fish boxes or suitcases arranged on the open deck. She made one round-trip daily between Ocracoke Island and the mainland port of Atlantic, North Carolina.

The mail boat left the island soon after daybreak and arrived at the dock in Atlantic about 10:30 a.m. The *Aleta* laid over long enough to load mail, passengers, and supplies. Shortly after noon she made her way back east across Pamlico Sound, riding low in the water. It was not unusual for all of the men on board to be asked, at least once, to jump overboard and push the old wooden boat off of a sandy shoal. The *Aleta* always arrived back home by late afternoon, safe and intact.

Mail Boat Aleta

At that time the main social event of the day was greeting the mail boat when it glided up to the dock about 4:30 p.m. It seemed as if the entire village was there waiting for the mail, wondering who was coming home for a visit, and curious to see if any strangers were aboard. Old ladies in slat bonnets, carrying baskets filled with groceries from the general store or vegetables from their gardens, waited alongside old men in slouch hats smoking cigars or chewing tobacco.

The atmosphere was congenial and jovial as adults shared the day's news and gossip. Teenage boys in bare feet, white t-shirts, and dungarees rolled up to their calves greeted the mail boat and eagerly hefted large canvas bags of mail over their shoulders and carried them down the dock to the waiting postmaster. Younger children squealed and ran about or entertained themselves chucking oyster shells into the harbor. Eventually the mail would be "called over" and everyone would return to their homes for supper.

One morning the manager's wife boarded the *Aleta* for a trip across the sound to visit family and friends. Several days later, at the time of her scheduled return, she was conspicuously absent among the passengers disembarking from the mail boat when it arrived back home at Ocracoke.

Meeting the Mail Boat

The manager seemed perplexed, but not overly concerned. No doubt his wife had decided to spend several more days with family and friends on the mainland, he thought. She would be home soon enough. In the meanwhile his life was calmer and more peaceful.

A week later, to everyone's horror, the woman's mutilated body was discovered on the mainland, the victim of a horrible murder. Lying face up in a pool of blood in an abandoned house, her throat had been cut. Although suspicion immediately centered on an unidentified serviceman who had been seen getting into a car with her, her murderer was never determined. Not surprisingly, many islanders wondered whether her husband had had something to do with the murder.

Already a heavy drinker, the manager relied increasingly on alcohol to dull his senses after his wife's funeral. He was never accused of the murder, and he returned to work at the Silver Lake Inn. Evenings and nights in his quarters became increasingly troubled. Almost immediately he began seeing his wife's ghost wandering the halls of the Inn.

All too often he would awake in the middle of the night to see her standing over his bed, fixing him with an accusing stare. She opened doors, and then abruptly slammed them closed. The stairs creaked and groaned as she made her way from floor to floor. He would enter his room to find his wife's cosmetics, left untouched on the dresser since her demise, now rearranged while he was out.

Eventually the distressed manager could endure no more. He quit his job at the Inn and moved back to the mainland. He never returned to Ocracoke.

Over the years reports have continued to surface of Mrs. Godfrey's ghost regularly patrolling rooms and hallways of the Island Inn. Most sightings have occurred on the second and third floors of the main section. It is not uncommon for guests who have never heard the story to approach the front desk in the morning with strange tales of doors opening and closing, of unfamiliar footsteps padding nearby in the middle of the night, or of bathroom spigots opening by themselves.

Women frequently report going out for dinner or a walk on the beach and returning to find their cosmetics scattered about on the dresser. One woman awoke with a start and was terrified to see a ghostly figure examining her toiletries. The next morning her makeup was gone. She never located it.

A young couple was staying at the Inn a number of years ago before the installation of air conditioning. The August evening was particularly hot and muggy. Not a breath of wind disturbed the heavy night air. Hoping for some relief, the couple stepped onto the balcony and settled into rockers. After a while the husband turned to his wife with a curious look on his face. "Did you just feel something odd?" he asked her. "I did," she replied. "All of a sudden I felt a cold ripple of air passing, not over me, but through me, as if something living, but not really living, had touched my soul." He had felt the same uneasy sensation.

The woman on my ghost tour repeats her story of feeling someone holding on to her big toe. She vows never to stay in the older section of the Inn again. Her voice betrays a lingering dread of unseen forces hovering over her bed. She is content, however, to rent a room in the newer wing, as she does often.

Only a few years ago I asked the current owners of the Island Inn if folks still report strange happenings in the upper floors of the main building.

"Oh, every summer we have at least half a dozen guests come downstairs in the morning and tell us about things they've heard or seen during the night. When we explain to them about the manager's wife they nod and admit they're not surprised."

"But there's more," she continues, clearly animated by her own experiences.

"We have a regular guest here who always brings her guitar. She comes several times a year and just loves staying with us. She claims she gets the best night's sleep in her room on the second floor. After one visit I found a small peg on the floor. It had a round, flattened end, but I didn't recognize what it was, so I threw it away. The next day it was lying on the floor in the hallway. I discarded it again. The third time I found it in the middle of the mirror-stand at the top of the stairs. By then it was beginning to feel creepy. I picked up the peg, carried it downstairs and tossed it into the waste basket.

"The guest called several days later. She had lost one of her guitar pegs, and wondered if we had found it. I explained what had happened and apologized. The peg was gone for good now, I explained.

"Weeks later the guitarist was back, anticipating another relaxing island weekend. Imagine my surprise when she came down to the main desk to thank me for the guitar pin. It was lying on the table in her room!"

"Let me tell you another story," the owner continues.

"One of our guests dropped her glasses just as she stepped out of her room, and onto the outside stairway. She searched ten minutes or more, but could not find her glasses. When she told us what had happened we went to help. The glasses had simply disappeared. Finally we gave up, and she checked out without her glasses.

"Two weeks went by, then one day another guest walked up to the counter with a pair of glasses. She found them lying on the steps, just outside her room. Sure enough, they were the missing glasses."

The ghost in the Island Inn often seems to be kind and nurturing. At least that's what people say. Some even claim that she tucks people in at night, and that is why they sleep so soundly.

She does like to play tricks, though, and has a fascination with jewelry. One woman, staying on the island while going through a difficult divorce, took off her wedding ring before going to court on the mainland. When she returned to the island her ring was gone. She never located it.

Not everyone who stays at the Island Inn encounters the ghost. Some are disappointed when she doesn't make herself known. Even when she does, she seems harmless enough to those who have felt her presence. If you're curious, you are invited to reserve a room at the Inn. We recommend you ask for room number 23 or 24.

THE TWO GUTS

MISS Sue Scarborough and her husband Charlie lived on a large lot near where the National Park Service Visitor Center stands today. The trim and tidy house, with two front gables and a comfortable front porch, is gone now, but the tiny Scarborough family cemetery lies not far from the Center, surrounded by a delicate white picket fence. Charlie's mother and father, Chloe Ann and Thaddeus, are buried there, along with Charlie's infant sister, Florence, and his infant brother, Neafie.

Charlie & Sue Scarborough House

Sue and Charlie's house was not far from Cockle Creek, nor from the shore of Pamlico Sound, and their three children learned early about life on an island. Fish and crabs were plentiful, and the family enjoyed them often for midday dinner. A white picket fence around their house helped contain the younger children just as surely as it kept the wild ponies from trampling their well-tended garden.

Neighbors were never very far away in this compact little village, and Miss Sue and Charlie visited regularly, often carrying a sweet potato pie or a large bowl of clam chowder to share with folks nearby.

Miss Sue's sister, Eliza (almost everyone called her Lyzee), had married a sailor, Captain William Thomas. Captain Thomas was in the Caribbean in the late nineteenth century and sailed into port at the exotically beautiful island of St. Kitts. There he noticed a tall two-story side gable house with a prominent center cross gable. All three gables were ornamented with pierced, sawtooth trim boards. The windows were protected from hurricane force winds by sturdy wooden shutters.

Captain Thomas took a special liking to this house and immediately made a sketch of it. On his return to Ocracoke he presented the sketch to his brother-in-law, Mr. Charlie, one of the island's most talented carpenters. Mr. Charlie agreed to build the house for his brother-in-law.

Captain Thomas made arrangements to have all of the lumber brought to the island, and Charlie commenced building without delay. He built the house for a mere fifty dollars.

Captain William & Eliza Thomas House

Not many months earlier the "Old August Storm" of 1899 had done considerable damage to many houses on Ocracoke Island. Mr. Charlie's house had the misfortune of being flooded by the rapidly rising tide. Typically, islanders reacted swiftly when high water threatened their property. Afraid that flood tides might lift their houses off their piers and float them away, most Ocracokers quickly took saws and drills and cut holes in their floors to allow seawater to rush inside their houses and alleviate the pressure under the sills. Not everyone had enough time to scuttle their floors, however, and some houses were destroyed after they floated into trees, boats, or other houses.

Troubled by recalling the destruction caused by the August storm, Mr. Charlie was determined that wouldn't happen to his brother- and sister-in-law. Captain Thomas and Miss Lyzee's house would have a proper trap door built into the floor to let the seawater in during a storm. This was the first house constructed on the island with such a trap door.

The Captain Thomas house sits on the south side of Cockle Creek, a striking landmark in spite of the destruction of its two-story porch during the hurricane of 1944. The gray batten shutters even today bear witness to the many storms that have assailed this historic structure, but it remains perched exactly where Mr. Charlie built it.

Miss Lyzee often climbed the stairs, looked out her window, and gazed across the water at her sister's house on the north side of Cockle Creek. But only rarely did they visit. When Miss Sue took a notion to visit Lyzee it was not an impulsive thought. She intended it to be a proper visit, and that meant spending enough time with her sister to make the trip worthwhile.

For you see, Miss Sue lived Around Creek and Miss Lyzee lived Down Point. So Miss Sue would pack her valise and make the long journey to her sister's on foot.

Today people who visit Ocracoke Island are often perplexed when they hear a native talk about living Around Creek or Down Point. Even for folks who have been coming to the island for years there are no obvious landmarks to identify these two major sections of tiny Ocracoke village which today meld seamlessly into each other.

Cockle Creek, ca. 1941

The creek side is the area on the north shore of Silver Lake Harbor (Cockle Creek) and includes the National Park Service Visitor Center, Howard Street, and the Methodist Church. The point side takes in Albert Styron's Store, the lighthouse and surrounding areas to the south.

The visitor might even detect a bit of good-natured competition between creekers and pointers. And it might take a while to understand the historical significance of the distinction. After all, Ocracoke is a small village that even today has a population of fewer than 800 people. The motivation for identifying with one half of the village or the other is a part of our local history.

Prior to World War II Silver Lake Harbor was generally referred to as Cockle Creek (or often just "the Creek"). Although a natural harbor, it was, and still is, a wide tidal creek that is joined to Pamlico Sound by a narrow inlet dubbed "the Ditch" by locals. Originally most of the periphery of the harbor was low, marshy, and wet, a perfect breeding ground for the ubiquitous Outer Banks mosquitoes.

The Creek was hardly more than three or four feet deep, unsuitable for any but the shallowest draft flat bottom skiffs. Many of these were tied to stobs near the shore where children caught pin fish in nets, or collected hermit crabs in buckets. On the east side, the Creek extended far into the village as a pair of narrow streams or guts that effectively divided Ocracoke village into two distinct areas.

One gut lay more or less where North Carolina Highway 12 now runs. This stream was narrower and shallower, hence the moniker, "Little Gut." Another, "Aunt Winnie's Gut," was situated farther south. This designation was not a statement about Aunt Winnie's size or shape. She simply lived next to the gut. This one was wider and deeper and was sometimes called simply the "Big Gut."

Aunt Winnie, as everyone called her, came to Ocracoke about 1865. From Blount's Creek in eastern North Carolina, she and her husband Harkus (or Hercules) were the only former slaves to settle on Ocracoke after President Lincoln issued his Emancipation Proclamation.

Prior to the Civil War a number of Ocracoke citizens had owned slaves. With the outbreak of hostilities all of the island's black population fled to the mainland. Although some islanders believe Aunt Winnie had lived on Ocracoke before the war, her granddaughter, Mildred Bryant, claimed not. According to older residents, Aunt Winnie and Harkus accompanied a Williams family to the island.

Over the years the Blounts lived in several small houses, including one on the sound shore. Eventually they settled on a large tract of land near the Big Gut. It remains a mystery exactly how they came in possession of this land.

Winnie and Harkus raised two children on Ocracoke, Elsie Jane and Anna Laura. Anna Laura married early, but the young couple moved away soon after their toddler drowned in an open water barrel. Jane married Leonard Bryant, a visiting laborer from Englehard, North Carolina. Together they raised nine children on Ocracoke. Their daughter Muzel Bryant, the last of her family to call Ocracoke home, died in 2008 at the age of 103.

The Bryants were pointers, and Aunt Winnie's Gut, as well as the Little Gut, were prominent landmarks for much of Ocracoke's history. Both guts extended from the Creek all the way to the bald beach.

For many years only primitive wooden foot bridges spanned the guts. Little more than wide planks resting on the banks of the streams, and propped on stumps in the water, the rickety bridges at least allowed foot passage from one side to the other.

In the age before paved roads it was a significant hike through soft sand paths from one side of the village to the other. The walk was even more difficult for islanders carrying a child, a laundry basket, a mess of collards from the garden, or even a small valise.

For a driver with horse and cart the trip was even more daunting. He was forced to detour around the guts by taking his team out to the bald beach and back up the other side of the village. It was a trip not lightly embarked on.

Although the village was geographically divided, most islanders, like Miss Sue and Miss Lyzee, were related in one way or another. They might live on opposite sides of the central harbor, and they might not visit back and forth often, but Ocracokers still understood that they formed one community. Even when squabbles erupted, or schoolchildren squared off on either side of one of the guts and dared their rivals to cross over, everyone still knew that working together was necessary in order to live comfortably and prosper.

By Miss Sue's and Miss Lyzee's time the education of all of Ocracoke's children was a primary concern of many islanders. Over the course of decades, beginning in the late 1700s, a number of private and public schools had been established on Ocracoke. Before the Civil War at least two schoolhouses stood on the island, one Around Creek, near the present-day British Cemetery, the other Down Point, about a quarter of a mile northeast of the lighthouse. Both schoolhouses were destroyed during the war, presumably by invading Union soldiers, but they were quickly rebuilt. Frequent storms caused more damage. A hurricane in the late nineteenth century even washed the southern schoolhouse to the opposite side of the road.

The "Old August Storm" of 1899, with winds of 120 miles an hour, caused considerable damage on Ocracoke Island. Describing the destruction on nearby Hatteras Island, S.L. Dosher, official Weather Bureau Observer, wrote, "Language is inadequate to express the conditions which prevailed all day on [August 17]. The howling wind, the rushing and roaring tide and the awful sea which swept over the beach and thundered like a thousand pieces of artillery made a picture which was at once appalling and terrible and the like of which Dante's *Inferno* could scarcely equal."

Ocracoke I.O.O.F. Lodge & Schoolhouse

Both schoolhouses were severely damaged in the Old August Storm, and many islanders soon began calling for one new schoolhouse.

At the turn of the twentieth century James and Zilphia Howard sold a one acre tract of their land to the trustees of "Ocracoke Lodge No. 194 Independent Order of Odd Fellows" for use as a "Lodge room or such other purpose as they may deem proper." A two story wood frame building was completed in 1901. It housed the Odd Fellow's Lodge on the second floor. Today this building serves as the main section of the Island Inn.

The Lodge was built directly between the two guts. Soon after its construction both island schools were abandoned and a new "consolidated" public school was established on the first floor of the lodge. Creekers and pointers were now all attending the same school.

Elizabeth Ann O'Neal was born in 1910, and lived Around Creek. At six years old she attended school in the Odd Fellows Lodge, but only for a short while.

Soon after Elizabeth's first day, her cousin Iola awoke in the middle of the night during a distressing dream. Iola had dreamt that Elizabeth, while walking to school, slipped on the bridge crossing one of the guts, muddy water. The dream felt so real, and it played over mind. Iola felt compelled to share the dream with Elizabe...

Native islanders always considered dreams powerful omens, and ... mother was no exception. She viewed Iola's nightmare as a "token of death." She was determined to heed its warning and thwart its prediction. She reacted immediately and removed her daughter from school. Elizabeth was privately tutored from that time on.

Bridge over the Gut

In the mid-1930s young men in the nation's Civilian Conservation Corps traveled to Ocracoke and participated in several public works projects. The best known of these endeavors was the construction of new, wider bridges to span the two guts. Islanders were delighted that the new bridges even had hand rails. At least one of the bridges was wide enough to take a cart, or even an automobile, across.

When the Navy established their World War II base on Ocracoke during the latter half of 1942 one of their first goals was to create a navigable, deep water harbor for their vessels.

The Creek had been partially dredged in the late 1930s. Once more the navy dredged Cockle Creek, this time to a depth of 15—20 feet. The protection afforded by Ocracoke's now deeper harbor allowed a significant and valuable naval presence to finally put an end to the carnage inflicted on allied merchant ships by German U-boats in the first six months of 1942.

Much of the dredged sand was pumped into the surrounding wetlands. The

₃es were dismantled and the guts filled in. Although locals still refer to the harbor as the Creek, after WWII this body of water, now a haven for all manner of sail and motor vessels, is routinely referred to by the more colorful name, Silver Lake.

Of course, there are no longer any guts to divide Ocracoke village. And no creeker even considers packing her bags to go Down Point to visit relatives for several days. But the terms creeker and pointer still live on, a subtle reminder of the way island life used to be.

A DISEMBODIED HEAD

A N attractive one-story turn-of-the-twentieth-century home sits on the southeast side of Lighthouse Road, about one-quarter mile from North Carolina Highway 12. With a hip roof, clapboard siding, wrap-around porch, two-over-two windows, turned porch posts, and a white picket fence, the James Henry Garrish home is a typical, if dwindling, example of old-time Ocracoke architecture.

James Henry Garrish

James Henry Garrish (1877-1947) was the great-great-grandson of Henry Garrish, one of Ocracoke's first settlers. Henry Garrish, who likely hailed from New England, made his living as a private tutor in the late 1700s. He was married to Elizabeth Howard, the daughter of William Howard Jr., son of the last colonial owner of Ocracoke Island.

There is nothing to suggest that Ocracoke had a schoolhouse or any type of public education at that time. But we can be certain that, for his time, Henry Garrish was a well-educated gentleman.

After James Henry's death in 1947 the home was sold out of the family. For a while it was used as a summer residence, but in the mid-1970s new island residents rented the house for their year-round home. As they established themselves in the community it became clear that they intended to remain on Ocracoke. In 1978 they had the opportunity to purchase an adjoining parcel of land. They moved an older island home from near the lighthouse to their new lot and began the lengthy process of repairing and restoring it.

Some years after they moved into their newly rehabilitated home the young couple had the opportunity to purchase the James Henry Garrish home also.

By then their family included children, and the James Henry Garrish house next door was put on the market as a weekly summer rental.

It was during this time that renters began reporting unusual occurrences in the house. They would arise in the morning to discover that pictures on the walls were hanging upside down. Sometimes they would see a short woman, her gray hair pinned up in a bun, a simple cotton apron wrapped around her waist, standing in the bedroom in the middle of the night. Guests would occasionally wake up from a sound sleep to see this ghostly figure pacing the room. She never spoke, but seemed intent on inspecting the new occupants and their belongings. In short order she would disappear as silently as she had materialized.

One summer night twin school-age sisters were sharing the center bedroom just off the main hallway. Aroused from her slumber, one of the twins opened her eyes to see an apparition standing at the foot of the bed staring intently into her eyes. The young girl nudged her sister awake and together they watched as the spectral woman smiled, then slowly dissolved and vanished into the heavy summer air.

More than occasionally renters would visit the realty office in the morning and report unusual feelings and frightening sightings at the James Henry Garrish home. Sometimes the experiences would be so disturbing that they would demand to be moved to another cottage.

Years before, during one remodeling of the house, an L-shaped addition of three rooms had been built onto the back of the house, and the porch was extended along the length of this addition and connected to the porch of the main house. Some time later the rear porch addition was enclosed and turned into a hallway. About this time the rear-most room of the L was converted into a kitchen.

As a result, it was no longer necessary to walk through the two "addition" rooms (now bedrooms) or outside onto an open porch in order to reach the kitchen in the rear of the house. The newly created hallway served this purpose. But this renovation made for an unusual feature, for now the windows in the two bedrooms no longer opened onto the porch, but onto an enclosed hallway.

James Henry Garrish House

In the 1980s a young man from the southwest had moved to Ocracoke for the summer. For a time he stayed in the James Henry Garrish home. His bedroom was located in the rear L. To him the house seemed saturated with history. Dents and scratches in the old pine floors were hieroglyphics that could tell him so much, if only he could decipher them. And the furniture! Whose clothes had rested, neatly folded, in those dresser drawers? The house seemed almost alive.

As so many other islanders, he routinely slept with the windows up and the curtains open. He enjoyed the sounds of the night – crickets and peepers, especially. Sometimes a colony of emerald green tree frogs could be deafening, particularly after a rainfall when they were courting. But mostly they seemed comforting. The low, mournful call of a hoot owl, however, rolling sonorously through the neighborhood on a moonlit night, could give him the willies.

Like others who lived in this house, he awoke one night (it was about 2 a.m.) with a sense of dread and unease. He tossed and turned, and gradually found himself lying in bed fully awake. Something was not right, he was certain, but he did not know what. Slowly the realization came over him. Someone was in the hallway, just outside his window.

Ocracoke is not known for burglars or other intruders. Islanders generally sleep soundly, safe in the knowledge that little crime occurs in this isolated village so far from mainland worries or concerns. Nevertheless, this young man felt increasingly uncomfortable and lay in bed for a time, uncertain what to do next.

He heard no sounds, no footfalls, no creaking floorboards, no squeaking hinges. But there was no doubt that someone, or something, was moving about in the hallway. He stared into the semi-darkness of the narrow hallway. Light from the waxing moon cast surreal shadows of ancient live oaks against the white bead board walls.

Suddenly he understood why he had felt such a sense of foreboding. Outside his bedroom window, floating silently and effortlessly down the enclosed hall, bobbed the pale white, disembodied head of an old woman. Like the other apparitions, her gray hair was pulled back in a severe bun, and her face was creased with wrinkles and deep lines.

She stopped at the open window and fixed him with her vacant eyes. For what seemed like minutes, she stared at him, and he stared back. Then suddenly the ghostly head was gone. A cold breeze rustled the curtains, the moon retreated behind a bank of storm clouds, and a light rain began to fall.

Morning did not come soon enough.

The owners' daughters, now grown, decided that they would probably never want to live in this haunted house. Today the Garrish home is owned by New Orleans natives who have been island residents for a number of years. The new owners have expressed few concerns about nighttime ghostly visitors. In 2005 they embarked on an ambitious project to rehabilitate their island home to North Carolina state historic preservation standards. In 2006 they moved into their "new" home.

Recently one of the current owners of the James Henry Garrish house stopped me along the road. She had heard numerous stories about her house. "I've never seen a ghost in this house...yet" she said, "but I must tell you...every morning when we get up many of the pictures on the walls are canted, and hanging at odd angles."

ISLAND SCHOOLHOUSES

MR. Rondthaler stepped onto the front porch and rang the brass school bell. Barefooted children from first graders to seniors tossed a ball one last time or allowed the swing to coast to a stop, then plucked sand spurs from their clothes and scurried back inside.

Recess was over.

A handful of older pupils filed into Mr. Deering's classroom. As in every other old building on Ocracoke the faint odor of mildew permeated the air. The teenagers took their seats behind worn oak desks with grooves for holding pencils and now-unused holes for ink bottles. Mr. Deering was sitting in his chair, the one that looked to be fifty years old, with legs that splayed out and were fitted with metal rollers. If he was careful, Mr. Deering could lean back, and the sturdy spring under the seat, the one with adjustable tension, would hold him in just the right position to keep him from scooting across the room.

Mr. Deering rose from his chair and addressed his charges. He explained the day's lesson, and handed out worksheets. As the students chatted and then extracted tired books from their desks he settled back into his chair and propped his feet up on his heavy oak desk. The bottom of each shoe had a large hole in it.

I don't believe it had anything to do with poverty, though I'm sure Ocracoke schoolteachers were not paid large salaries in the late 1950s. Shoes, like almost everything else, were not easy to come by back then. Islanders ordered most of what they needed from mail-order catalogs, and sometimes it just took a while to get around to placing the order. Then, of course, you'd have to wait for your merchandise to arrive from the mainland store by mail boat.

During those years Ocracoke was one of the most laid-back villages in the nation. Even schoolteachers had no need for pretension. If your shoes had holes in them nobody seemed to care. Besides, most of the students were barefooted. Some even rode their horses to school.

But Ocracoke School was blessed by outstanding teachers, particularly the

Rondthalers. Theodore Rondthaler, North Carolina native and son of a Moravian bishop, accepted the position of principal in 1948. His wife, Alice, came along as a teacher, and together they taught on the island for fourteen years.

Both Alice and Theodore had a knack for teaching, in a manner that respected their charges and their heritage, and encouraged learning. A former student tells of the time one of the older children came into Mr. Rondthaler's class and used one of the cruder words in the English language…and used it incorrectly. Instead of berating the young man, Mr. Rondthaler created an opportunity for learning. "If you are going to use words like that," Theodore explained, "then you are going to learn to use them correctly." With that he launched into a lesson about verb conjugation using the usually forbidden word as an example.

The Rondthalers were part of a long tradition dedicated to the education of island youth. Information about the very first schools on Ocracoke Island is scarce, and what is available is often confusing. The first mention of formal schooling occurs in 1785 when Henry Garrish was hired as tutor for the young Thomas Wahab.

The first schoolhouse was not built until several years later, and over the succeeding years several projects were undertaken to provide island children with formal education. The community came together in the 1820s to finance a new school, and by the time of the Civil War Ocracoke had two public schoolhouses, one Down Point, and one Around Creek.

Private ventures also offered book learning to island boys and girls. Just three years after Lee surrendered at Appomattox a young islander opened her "Select School" for twelve eager pupils. In the late 1800s a tutor was hired to instruct children of the life savers stationed at Cedar Hammock, near Hatteras Inlet. At least one other private school was established in the village.

Between 1881 and 1901 several attempts were made to improve public education on Ocracoke, but efforts were thwarted by a lack of finances, destruction of facilities during storms and hurricanes, and disagreements among island officials. Finally, in 1901 a new building was constructed by the recently established fraternal organization, the Independent Order of Odd Fellows, and public school for the entire village was opened on the ground floor.

In 1917 formal instruction of island children was moved to a handsome new schoolhouse that was built where the present schoolhouse now sits. Over the years many improvements have been made to the education of Ocracoke's youth.

As of this writing, more than a dozen teachers instruct children from pre-kinder-garten to twelfth grade in facilities constructed between 1971 and 2006.

Total enrollment at Ocracoke School, even today, is seldom much more than 100 students, although teachers and staff number significantly more than the two or three teachers Ocracoke School sometimes had in the past.

Even in the twenty-first century Ocracoke remains an informal village. Students no longer ride horses to school, and regulations now require them to wear shoes, but still no one cares if the teachers have holes in the bottoms of their shoes.

(Readers who would like a more detailed account of island schools are referred to Appendix I at the end of the book.)

BUNIA FOSTER AND THE BALL OF LIGHT

IN middle age Homer Howard (1868—1947) enlisted in the U.S. Life Saving Service. His father, James Howard, had served from 1883 until 1903 as keeper of the first Ocracoke Life Saving Station at Cedar Hammock, not far from Hatteras Inlet. Captain Jim, as he was known, and his crew of a half dozen surfmen were instrumental in saving the lives of hundreds of sailors whose vessels fetched up on Ocracoke's beach in the late nineteenth century.

Cedar Hammock LSS, ca. 1895

Although Homer had tried his hand at operating a general store on the island, seafaring was in his blood.

As a young man he had gone to sea, one of many islanders who made their living as sailors. While serving aboard a coastal schooner the vessel was overtaken by a menacing black thunder squall. Unable to outrun the front, the schooner was beset with violent winds and heavy seas that crashed upon the deck, threatening to dismantle the rigging and send boat, crew, and cargo to the bottom of the sea. In one horrifying instant, Homer was washed overboard when a monstrous wave raced across the exposed deck. His shipmates were convinced they would never see him again. Miraculously, the next frothing wave washed him back onto the pitching deck.

Back home after surviving the terrible storm, and determined to spend more time with his family, but not relishing the uneventful life of a landlubber, Homer applied for a position in the U.S. Life Saving Service. He traveled off the island to the nearest recruiting office.

Homer Howard

After Homer's interview he was ushered into a waiting room with several other would-be recruits. The chief officer, a rotund man who bobbed up and down as he walked, stepped into the room to speak briefly with the aspiring surfmen. After several minutes the officer stepped back into his adjacent office.

Thinking the officer was out of earshot, Homer turned to the youth sitting next to him. "That captain there," he whispered, nodding his head toward the other room, "looks like one of those big can buoys out in the inlet, don't you think?"

In an instant Homer regretted his indiscretion, for the captain had quietly re-entered the waiting room just in time to overhear what Homer had said. He demanded that Homer repeat his comment. Homer reluctantly complied. With a stern look and an admonition to keep such thoughts to himself in the future, the captain explained that such insubordinate comments were not to be tolerated in government service.

In spite of Homer's faux pas he was accepted into the Life Saving Service. One of his assignments was at the Little Kinnakeet Station on Hatteras Island.

By then he and his wife, Aliph O'Neal Howard, had had nine children. Although several died at birth or shortly thereafter, five children were living when Aliph discovered that she was pregnant once again. Aliph's Ocracoke O'Neal family, from old world Irish stock, commonly sported red hair and freckles. Homer's friends back on Ocracoke had routinely teased him with each pregnancy, predicting that his next Howard baby would be red-headed. And at each birth Homer breathed a sigh of relief when the newborn arrived with dark hair and showed more affinity to the Howard clan than to the O'Neals.

It was 1911 and Aliph was nearing term. Homer vowed that if his new baby was red-headed he would be forced to abandon it on Hatteras Island.

Shortly thereafter Lawton Wesley Howard was born in Homer and Aliph's modest home on Hatteras. He was the first of their children to sport bright orange-red hair.

Not long after Lawton's birth Homer had an opportunity to transfer and to continue his service back home at the Ocracoke Station. He had made arrangements with another surfman on Ocracoke to trade places. To move back to the island meant facing his friends with a baby who looked like an O'Neal. What was Homer to do?

Homer, Aliph, and the children would be leaving in the morning. Homer decided that, as much as he hated to do it, he had only one option.

In the middle of the night, while Aliph slept, Homer tiptoed to the washstand and picked up his straight razor. He ran his thumb along the blade. It was sharp enough to do the job, and do it quickly.

Homer picked up the sleeping baby (he was so small they had placed him in a dresser drawer). Silently, and with a few deft strokes Homer shaved Lawton's head bald.

They could now return home.

A few years after arriving back on Ocracoke, in 1915, the United States Congress merged the Life Saving Service with the Revenue Cutter Service to form the U.S. Coast Guard.

Most stations on the Outer Banks were built about fourteen miles apart. The typical method of patrolling the beach involved two surfmen. One would leave each station and walk towards the other one. When they met they would exchange tokens or "punch a clock" as proof that the entire length of the beach had been covered.

The first Life Saving Station on Ocracoke Island was established at Hatteras Inlet in 1883. In 1904 a second station was built in the village of Ocracoke. To ensure a timely response in the event of a shipwreck each surfman on beach patrol was eventually allowed to take his horse with him. He was required to walk until a wreck had been sighted. Then he was expected to mount his horse and ride to the nearest station as quickly as possible to sound the alarm.

One evening in November of 1928, while on patrol, Homer saw a mysterious ball of light floating in the crisp night air, just ahead of him, and not far above the hard-packed beach. Immediately he mounted his steed in an attempt to approach this unusual object. To his dismay, as he neared, the ball of light moved farther away. He spurred his horse, trying to catch up to the unnatural object, but the faster he traveled, the faster the apparition sped ahead of him.

Homer was determined. Driving his horse, he followed the light for miles. As the light approached the south point of beach it turned sharply and moved toward the village. In those days little vegetation separated the bald beach from houses lining the main road (now named Lighthouse Road).

All the way into the village Homer followed the light. To his surprise it stopped just outside the upstairs window of the home of Zion Foster and his sister, Bunia, across the street from Albert Styron's general store. Homer was glad to end his pursuit and rest his horse, but worried about what this omen might portend. As Homer watched in amazement, the light hovered, then suddenly passed through the window glass and was gone.

Homer sat in his saddle and gazed up at the window. It was late by now, and with the ball of light no longer visible, the velvety black sky seemed alive with innumerable stars, sparkling like so many diamonds above the treetops.

What was he to make of this strange occurrence? He needed time to think. Turning his horse back to the beach he continued his patrol with only half of his usual attention. Fortunately, the ocean was quiet that night. He sighted not a single vessel offshore. That was good. He had time to wonder, and contemplate what exactly he had seen.

Before returning to the station Homer stopped by his home, dismounted, and stepped inside. Quietly he opened the bedroom door and gently put his hand on Aliph's shoulder.

Aliph awoke and listened to Homer's story without saying a word. Both knew that for generations islanders had recounted similar stories, stories of eerie "tokens of death," many times involving mysterious balls of light.

USLSS Quarters

In fact, Christoph von Graffenried, in his *Account of the Founding of New Bern* [North Carolina], recounts a "marvellous" event that took place while he was being held captive by a band of Tuscarora Indians in early September of 1711. According to him, a deceased widow was being buried, and the natives were performing their rituals over the grave when "[a] pretty fire or flame of about two candle light size went straight up into the air, as high probably, as the longest and tallest tree, traveled again in a straight line over the hut of the deceased and so farther over a great heath, probably half an hour long until it disappeared in a forest."

Homer and Aliph talked for some time, wondering what Homer's encounter meant, especially for the Fosters. But they could only speculate. There was nothing to do that late in the night.

And so it was that Homer, his duty complete, rode back to the Coast Guard station, and Aliph settled down again in her bed. But neither of them slept soundly that night.

Homer awoke early the next morning, still perplexed by what he had seen the night before. Around the breakfast table he told his story to his fellow surfmen. Everyone listened with full attention. It was only a matter of time before they might learn the meaning of this strange sighting.

The news arrived by mid-morning. Bunia Foster had died during the night. Her brother discovered her lifeless body just after daybreak. The word spread quickly through the village. It was a shock to everyone except Homer and Aliph. Once again a token of death had announced the departure of one of Ocracoke's own.

THE OCRACOKE LIGHTHOUSE

OCRACOKE'S 77' tall white tower with a steady beam is the island's most recognizable landmark. Built in 1823 by Noah Porter of Massachusetts for $11,359.35 (this included the one-story keeper's quarters), the Ocracoke Lighthouse is actually one of five lights that have guided mariners through the often treacherous Ocracoke Inlet and surrounding shallow waters.

Ocracoke Lighthouse

In 1715 the North Carolina colonial assembly passed an act to settle and maintain pilots at Ocracoke Inlet. Knowledgeable locals familiar with the shallow Pamlico Sound and the ever-shifting channels, shoals, and sandbars were necessary to protect shipping interests to and from mainland North Carolina ports.

Because pirate captain Edward Teach and numerous other buccaneers had made Ocracoke Island a haven for outlaw sailors, few law-abiding colonists were brave enough to settle on this remote and isolated spit of sand in the early eighteenth century. For decades ship captains sailed through Ocracoke Inlet and across Pamlico Sound as best they could, without help from local pilots.

No one knows for sure when the first Europeans permanently settled on the island. However, Ocracoke was considered a town by 1753, and virtually all of the original male residents were pilots.

In 1789 the North Carolina General Assembly, recognizing that even more needed to be done to help ensure mariners' safety in the vicinity of Ocracoke Inlet, passed legislation to erect a lighthouse on Ocracoke.

Because of the concerns of local pilots and merchants, as well as owners and captains of vessels that used Ocracoke Inlet, the lighthouse was instead built on nearby Shell Castle Rock, just inside Ocracoke Inlet. This relatively stable 25 acre island of oyster shells was developed in 1789 by John Blount and John Wallace. At one time as many as 40 people lived and worked there, among docks, warehouses, at least one small store, modest homes, and even a wind-powered grist mill.

Congress authorized this first beacon in 1794, but it was not illuminated until 1803. According to a deed from J.G. Blount and John Wallace of February 7, 1795 for "land necessary for a lighted beacon on Shell Castle Island" it is stipulated that "no goods should be stored, no tavern be kept, no spirits be retailed, no merchandise be carried on, and that no person should reside on, or make it a stand to pilot or lighter vessels" on the land set aside for this lighthouse.

The lighthouse was a 55' wooden, pyramid-shaped tower covered with cedar shingles and erected on a sturdy stone foundation. Atop the tower was a six-foot lantern and a three-foot dome. The builder of this lighthouse was Henry Dearborn, who also built the first Cape Hatteras Lighthouse. Light was provided by one large whale oil lamp with four wicks.

The lighthouse is shown on an 1805-1810 pitcher (on display at the North Carolina Museum of History in Raleigh) bearing an image of Shell Castle. This is the earliest known image of a North Carolina lighthouse, and the only surviving depiction of this early nineteenth century beacon and the business complex on Shell Castle Island.

Almost immediately after it was completed the Shell Castle Light was made ineffective for navigation due to the ever-changing channels and shoals. By 1806 the channel had moved so far that the lighthouse was almost totally useless. Construction of a new tower was authorized. On August 16, 1818 lightning claimed the original structure and the keeper's quarters before a new tower could be built.

Not quite two years later, on May 15, 1820, funds were appropriated to station a light ship in Ocracoke Inlet. This proved inadequate for its purposes, and after two more years $20,000 was approved for the construction of the present Ocracoke Lighthouse. Jacob Gaskill, Justice of the Peace, sold the two acre parcel of land for the lighthouse to the government for fifty dollars on December 5, 1822.

Ocracoke Lighthouse stands 77 feet tall and tapers from a diameter of 25 feet at the base to 12 feet at the top. The tower's solid brick walls are five feet thick at the bottom and two feet thick at the top. An octagonal lantern housing the light sits atop the historic structure.

Ocracoke's Fresnel Lens

When first built, the lighthouse utilized a system of silvered reflectors to magnify the flame from a whale oil lamp. In 1854 a newly introduced Fresnel lens replaced the old system. Augustin Fresnel, a Frenchman, had invented a marvelous array of hand-cut glass prisms and bulls-eye lenses in 1822. The new lens magnified and intensified the Ocracoke light so that it was now equal to 8,000 candlepower and was visible 14 miles to sea. Later, different fuel oils were used, and finally, in 1929, the oil lamp was replaced by an incandescent bulb.

The present-day 250 watt quartz-halogen marine bulb is barely larger than the last two joints of a little finger. Four identical bulbs rest at ninety degree angles in a sophisticated lampchanger that automatically rotates to a new position when the top active bulb burns out. The lamp is activated by a light sensor and can be monitored remotely. A backup generator helps ensure a steady beam under virtually any conditions.

There are six sizes, or orders, of Fresnel lenses. Ocracoke's Fresnel lens is fourth-order. Sixth-order lenses are the weakest, and are generally used on lakes and harbors. First-order lenses are the strongest, and are used along the most treacherous coasts.

Fort Ocracoke

From 1853 to 1861 another lighthouse operated on nearby Beacon Island, just a short distance from Ocracoke, in Pamlico Sound. This beacon was 39 feet high. By 1857 it was considered useless, again due to the shifting channels. The same fate befell a new lightship that was installed near Ocracoke Inlet at about the same time.

In 1861, to protect ports, harbors, and shipping along the North Carolina coast from Union attacks, a small fort was built on Beacon Island. Construction was begun on March 20, the very day that North Carolina seceded from the Union. Ten days later Fort Ocracoke, as it was called, with several guns mounted on its earthen embankments (and more scheduled to be mounted in the next few days) was nearly completed.

In late August nearby Fort Hatteras and Fort Clark were captured by Union troops. With Fort Ocracoke still lacking necessary supplies, and with no more than a skeleton force, the Confederate defenders abandoned Beacon Island. When Union troops under the command of Lt. J.G. Maxwell on the gunboat *USS Pawnee,* along with the gunboat *USS Fanny,* arrived at Fort Ocracoke in September they discovered the fort deserted. Fearing future Confederate activity in the area Maxwell's forces disabled all of the guns as well as the beacon.

An excellent description of the fort is related in the following report made by Lieutenant Maxwell of the Union Steamer *Pawnee,* and found in the *Rebellion Records 1860-61* (paragraph spacing has been added for ease of reading):

UNITED STATES STEAMER PAWNEE HATTERAS INLET, SEPT. 18TH

Sir: I have to report that, in compliance with your orders of the 16th, I started for Ocracoke on that day, in the Fanny, towing the Pawnee's launch. Lieutenant Eastman had charge of the latter, with twenty-two men and six marines from the ship, and twenty-pound howitzer, and I had on board six men and sixty-one soldiers of the Naval Brigade, under Lieutenants Tillotson and Roe.

We arrived within two miles of the fort on Beacon Island at 11 o'clock A.M. when the Fanny grounded. I sent Lieutenant Eastman in the launch to sound for the channel. While he was so occupied, a sailboat with two men put off from Portsmouth to cross the sound. A shot from the Fanny brought them along side, and they piloted us to within an hundred yards of the fort.

It is called Fort Ocracoke, and is situated on the seaward of Beacon Island. It was entirely deserted. It is octagonal in shape, contains four shell rooms, about twenty five feet square, and in the center a large Bomb-proof, one hundred feet square, with the magazine within it. Directly above the magazine, on each side, were four large tanks containing water. The fort had been constructed with great care, of sand in barrels covered with earth and turf. The inner framing of the bomb-proof was built of heavy pine timbers.

There were platforms for twenty guns, which had been partly destroyed by fire. The gun carriages had been all burned. There were eighteen guns in the fort—namely, four eight inch navy shell guns, and fourteen long thirty-two pounders.

The steamer ALBEMARLE LEFT ON Sunday afternoon, carrying off two guns. I found one hundred and fifty barrels. Also, many of them filled with water. There being no water in the fort, they had brought it from Washington and Newberry.

I landed the men at half-past one o'clock, and commenced breaking off the trunnions of the guns. While a portion of our men and the Naval Brigade were so employed, I sent Lieutenant Eastman in the launch to Portsmouth, where he found three eight-inch navy shell guns lying on the beach and one mounted on a carriage. They had all been spiked. There was no battery erected there, although we were informed that one would have been built but for our coming.

There had been a camp at Portsmouth called Camp Washington, but a portion of the troops were sent to Fort Hatteras when it was attacked on August 28, and the remaining retired to the mainland. Portsmouth, which formerly contained four hundred and fifty inhabitants, was nearly deserted, but the people are expected to return. Those remaining seem to be Union men, and expressed satisfaction at our coming. Lieutenant Eastman assured them that they would not be molested by the government and that they might return to their usual occupations.

There are no entrenchments nor guns at Ocracoke. The fishermen and pilots, who fled after our attack, have generally returned. I tried to destroy the guns by breaking the trunnions off with sledge and by dropping solid shot upon them from an elevation, but with little success. I then tried solid shot from a sixty-four-pounder at them and in this manner disabled them. Lieutenant Eastman disabled the guns at Portsmouth by knocking off the cascables, and leaving them in the salt water on the beach.

After destroying the guns, I collected all the lumber, barrels and wheelbarrows, and placed them in and about the bomb-proof, set fire to the pile and entirely destroyed it. A lightship which had been used as a store ship, and which was run upon the shore some distance from the fort, with the intention of subsequently towing her off and arming, I set fire to.

At half-past six o'clock this morning I started on our return. We met with no detention, and arrived safely with all hands at half-past 11 o'clock. I am happy to report that the conduct of our men and the naval Brigade was excellent. Lieutenant Eastman and Lieutenant Tillotson and Lieutenant Roe of the Naval Brigade, rendered me most efficient assistance.

I am, respectfully, your obedient servant,
JAMES Y. MAXWELL
Lieutenant United States navy

Lighthouse Stairway

Ocracoke village saw little more action during the war, although Confederate troops removed the lens and other apparatus from the Ocracoke Lighthouse in 1862 to hamper Union navigation. Less than two years later the lens was reinstalled and the lamp relit.

In 1867 the lamp fuel was changed from whale oil to lard oil; in 1878 kerosene replaced lard oil. In 1897 the second story was added to the keeper's quarters. Two years later, because it was brighter and burned more efficiently, a new Franklin lamp replaced the old valve lamp inside the lens. The light was electrified in 1929, and in the same year another section was added to the keeper's quarters.

About 1950 the original wooden spiral stairway that was attached to the inside brick wall was replaced with the current metal stairwell that is supported by a center post. Throughout the succeeding years minor additions, improvements, repairs, and alterations were made to the tower, keeper's quarters, grounds, outbuildings, and walkways.

According to island native Ellen Marie Fulcher Cloud, no one seems to know who the first of Ocracoke's lighthouse keepers were. Extant records do not begin until 1847. Traditional keepers were appointed regularly until 1955. The light was fully automated in 1946.

Known lighthouse keepers include:

John Harker, 1847—1853
Thomas Styron, 1853—1860
William J. Gaskill, 1860—1862
Enoch Ellis Howard 1862—1897
J. Wilson Gillikin 1897—1898
Tillmon F. Smith 1898—1910
A.B. Hooper 1910—1912
Leon Wesley Austin 1912—1929
Joe Burrus 1929—1946
Clyde Farrow 1948—1955

In addition to ensuring that the beacon was maintained in good repair and illuminated at the proper times, the keeper also tended to the grounds and other structures. The U.S. Lighthouse Board even specified a whitewash recipe for keeping the tower protected and presentable:

One half bushel of unslaked lime with boiling water
One peck of salt
One half pound of powdered Spanish whiting [chalk, or calcium carbonate]
Three pounds of rice in boiling water
One pound of clear glue
The mixture was to be applied as hot as possible.

Because of the efforts of dedicated keepers, the Ocracoke Lighthouse, the oldest North Carolina lighthouse still in continuous service, has been maintained and preserved as a navigation aid for 185 years.

It is the second oldest operating lighthouse in the United States. The beacon still in use at Sandy Hook, New Jersey is the oldest, built in 1764. The Sambro Lighthouse in Nova Scotia, Canada, built in 1760, is the oldest operating lighthouse in North America.

Because of the narrow, nearly vertical ladder that leads into the lantern, the small confined space around the light and lens, the fragile brick walls and spiral staircase, as well as other architectural features, the lighthouse is not open to the public for climbing.

Keeper Enoch Ellis Howard tended to the Ocracoke Lighthouse for thirty-five years, longer than any other individual. He died on the property during his term of service, in 1897.

Although the lighthouse and keeper's quarters are probably the oldest structures on the island, stories of ghosts, hauntings, and other unusual activity have not been passed down. This may be because the lighthouse is government, not private, property, and keepers typically served a dozen years or fewer, and then moved on. Enoch Ellis Howard is the only person known to have died there.

Unlike a family home that was occupied by generations of the same family, where children and elders lived and died, the lighthouse property was seldom witness to visits from the Grim Reaper. No one is buried on the property.

A Haunted Cottage

This is not the case for a small bungalow only a short distance from the lighthouse. By the 1980s this family home had been converted to a rental cottage. A couple with two small children had rented the house for a week's vacation. An island family lived next door.

The young island mother had left her children at home with a baby sitter for the evening while she went to work at a local restaurant. Sometime after dark the mother received a worried call from her baby sitter. The people from the rental cottage had come over with disturbing news.

They had finished supper early, then repaired to the living room to play games with their children. By nightfall they were getting the children into their pajamas and readying them for bed. While the mother was reading her children a bedtime story, then singing them a familiar lullaby, she was aware of the soft sound of children's weeping coming from somewhere outside the window. After her charges had fallen asleep the weeping became plaintive wailing, and increased in intensity.

The pitiful cries of children had so disturbed them, and had continued for such a period of time, that the parents decided to walk outside to investigate. They could no longer ignore the incessant wailing. Could it be, they wondered, that one or more children were lost and wandering nearby, looking for their parents?

Oddly, the cries stopped when they stepped into the yard. After careful investigation they determined that the sound of the children must have been coming from farther away.

Not long after they went back inside, the cries began anew. This time they decided to pay a visit next door. After several days on the island they knew that a family with small children was living in the adjacent house. The crying must be coming from there, they thought.

They knocked on the door and the baby sitter invited them inside. The baby sitter was surprised by their story. She had not heard the crying, and her charges, as the neighbors were welcome to observe, were already sound asleep in their beds. They had gone to bed more than an hour earlier. Together, the adults investigated outside once again, but no one heard anything.

After the neighbors returned to their cottage, the baby sitter decided to give the young mother a call at work. Perhaps she had some insight, or could even come home for a few minutes to help search for these elusive wailing children.

Sufficiently disturbed by the unusual story, the young mother hurried home, only to discover the renters frantically throwing suitcases into the trunk of their car. The plaintive crying was unending, they explained, but only when they were inside the house. It was too much to endure. Whatever else it was, they were convinced that it was unnatural. The only children in their cottage were their own, and they, too, were fast asleep. They would be moving to a motel for the rest of the night.

It was then that the young island mother noticed the disturbed soil in the side yard. Only that afternoon a contractor had brought in a front end loader and back hoe to install a new septic field. In the process he had unearthed previously unknown graves of two small children.

After careful inquiry islanders recalled that many years ago the toddlers had died of common childhood diseases, and had been laid to rest in the side yard with handmade wooden boards to mark their graves.

Over time the markers had rotted away, and only a few older residents remembered the story...until the bones were discovered that summer day.

After hearing the explanation the renters never wavered in their resolve to find another place to spend their vacation.

Since then the house has sometimes been rented by the week, and sometimes year-round by the month. Periodically those who stay in the house report the strange wailing cries of young children, although never as persistent as that first night. Others claim to have seen the ghost of a large woman with her hair fastened behind her neck with long hair pins, some think the children's mother, wandering sadly through the house.

Whatever the explanation, the ghostly sounds and spectral visions are always accompanied by the soft, eerie glow of the light from the island's oldest structure, the stately Ocracoke Lighthouse.

SPRINGER'S POINT

S PRINGER'S Point juts out from the southwest shore of Ocracoke village like the knuckle on a bent thumb. Although a prominent, heavily wooded landmark when seen from Pamlico Sound, Springer's is often overlooked by the casual visitor to the island. From the village there is no road to take you to the Point; only a narrow footpath that leads through thickets of yaupon, myrtle and cedar to forty-two acres of impressive, undeveloped maritime forest.

Springer's Point

Springer's Point remains one of the last natural treasures within Ocracoke village. In 2004 the North Carolina Coastal Land Trust was successful in purchasing thirty-one acres of the Point. The preservation of this substantial portion of Springer's Point highlights the natural and historic significance of this area.

In the early eighteenth century Ocracoke Island was used chiefly by non-resident mainland colonists for grazing cattle, sheep, and other livestock.

An important navigable deep water channel passes close to the southwest shoreline, near Springer's Point. It was here that some of the first permanent residents built modest homes. As early as 1715 the colonial assembly recognized the need for establishing pilots on Ocracoke Island. They were to be responsible for seeing that vessels bound for the mainland were guided through the narrow channels between the numerous shoals. The assembly therefore passed an act for "settling and maintaining Pilots at...Ocacock Inlett." The settlement was dubbed Pilot Town but there is no evidence that pilots actually settled there until sometime in the 1730s.

Although much of the low-lying shoreline has succumbed to erosion over the years, today Springer's Point is thickly covered with ancient, gnarled live oaks, and numerous other trees and plants indigenous to Ocracoke and the Outer Banks. Standing underneath the canopy of branches and year-round foliage, especially at daybreak or dusk, leaves one with a sense of quiet awe and timeless wonder.

Under the canopy a path leads through a tunnel of thick growth onto a narrow, sandy beach where the clear water from Pamlico Sound laps against the seaweed-strewn shoreline. The sky can be bright here, looking out towards the distant horizon. Just under the gently breaking waves lie numerous broken shells.

Old Pipe Bowls

Sometimes a lucky beachcomber is rewarded with a piece of crockery or other man-made artifact. I once retrieved a small, primitive clay pipe bowl from the water along Springer's Point. Others have reported finding arrowheads left behind by Ocracoke's earliest adventurers. No evidence exists to indicate that Native Americans ever established a permanent settlement on Ocracoke Island. However, they must have frequented the island, especially the area around Springer's Point, gathering clams, oysters, crabs, and fish, all of which are abundant in the nearby waters.

Just offshore, hardly more than a clamshell's throw away, is Teach's Hole. This channel connects the Atlantic Ocean and Ocracoke Inlet with the deeper waters of Pamlico Sound. Edward Teach, better known as Blackbeard the Pirate, frequented these waters during his brief career. This was Blackbeard's favorite anchorage. From one of the higher dunes, or from the trees on shore, it would have been possible to spy any ships approaching Ocracoke Inlet.

In October of 1718, in the vicinity of Springer's Point, Captain Blackbeard hosted one of the largest gatherings of pirates ever to be held on the North American continent. Teach, along with pirate captains Israel Hands, Charles Vane, Robert Deal, and John Rackham, partied for several days along with their motley crews. Rum flowed freely, and hogs and cows were butchered and barbecued on the open beach.

It was also at Teach's Hole channel, only one month later, on November 22, 1718, that Blackbeard met his fate in a fierce battle with Lt. Robert Maynard of the Royal Navy. Because North Carolina's governor, Charles Eden, was doing little or nothing to halt piratical activity off his coast, Virginia's Governor Alexander Spotswood took the matter into his own hands and sent Lt. Maynard in pursuit of the dastardly pirate.

During the battle the decks were running with blood and the air was thick with gunpowder smoke. Blackbeard himself was wounded twenty-five times. Towards the end of the fighting Blackbeard nearly dispatched his adversary. A mighty blow from Teach's cutlass severed Maynard's sword at the hilt. As Maynard stepped back to regain some advantage, Blackbeard moved in for the kill. At that fateful moment one of Maynard's sailors, a Scotsman, approached the villain from behind and, with a mighty slice of his sword, severed the buccaneer's fearsome head from his powerful body.

And thus the Golden Age of Piracy came to an end.

After the battle Maynard hung Blackbeard's head from the bowsprit of his sloop, then sailed for Bath, North Carolina, where Blackbeard had established a home. In January of 1719, with his grisly trophy still hanging from the bowsprit, Maynard sailed to Williamsburg, Va. In early February he arrived in Norfolk. Around the middle of the month authorities in Hampton, Va. hanged many of Blackbeard's crew. The pirate captain's head was stuck on a pole at the entrance to the harbor, a grim warning to Teach's Brethren of the Coast.

Robert E. Lee, former North Carolina law professor, in his definitive book, *Blackbeard the Pirate, A Reappraisal of His Life and Times*, relates that "according to the legends of Virginia and the statements of a number of writers, Blackbeard's skull dangled from a high pole on the west side of the mouth of the Hampton River for many years as a warning to seafarers. The place is still known as 'Blackbeard's Point.'"

Before departing from North Carolina's Pamlico Sound, Maynard and his crew unceremoniously tossed the buccaneer's headless corpse overboard where it reportedly swam around the ship seven times before sinking into the murky depths. The legend is an eerie reminder that Edward Teach was bigger than life itself.

Even today, the spirit of Edward Teach lives on in the consciousness of those brave enough to visit the area near his watery grave, especially after dark. It is not uncommon for visitors to Springer's Point to report seeing unusual lights on the water or among the trees and bushes nearby. Rustling of tree limbs, and other odd movements, as well as unidentified sounds, often seem to emanate from within the otherwise protected confines of Springer's Point. More than one person has reported feeling the presence of Blackbeard's ghost pacing the narrow shoreline, searching in vain for his head.

According to Lee, "[i]n time, someone in Virginia took down the grim souvenir [Blackbeard's severed head] and fashioned [the skull] into the base of a large punch bowl." He goes on to recount that for many years the bowl rested in the Raleigh Tavern in Williamsburg, Virginia, where it was used as a drinking vessel. This information comes from the 1898 *Annals of Philadelphia and Pennsylvania Volume II*, by John F. Watson who states that the skull "was enlarged with silver...and I have seen those whose forefathers have spoken of their drinking punch from it; with a silver ladle appurtenant to that bowl."

Legends also suggest that for many years the skull made the rounds of coastal dinner parties as a sober reminder of the fate of lawless sailors. Other tales claim that the skull played a central role in fraternity rituals in both Virginia and Connecticut.

In a footnote in Lee's 1974 book he states that the skull can no longer be located in Virginia, although "a well-known New England writer on pirates and a collector of pirate memorabilia" claimed to be in possession of the famous skull.

The New England writer and collector Lee refers to is no doubt Edward Rowe Snow (1902-1982). A page from his out-of-print book, *Secrets of the North Atlantic Islands*, published in 1950, shows a picture of a skull. The caption reads, "The skull of the famous pirate Blackbeard, photographed with one of his pistols."

After his death, Snow's widow claimed to still be in possession of Captain Teach's skull. Eventually she donated the skull to the Peabody Essex Museum in Salem, Massachusetts.

The existence of two small graveyards at Springer's Point only adds to the uneasiness people feel there. Although this area was quite busy during the early history of Ocracoke Island, today it holds little more than memories. Only one stone marker remains from the early period, that of Daniel Tolson who died in 1879. Other unmarked graves are surely located in the area. Set on a narrow ridge, Tolson's gravesite is extremely difficult to find. After trudging through wet, marshy lowland and then pushing through thorns, briars, and thick underbrush one is finally rewarded with the sight of a single marble headstone on the edge of a small grassy clearing.

E.D. Springer

From 1759, when William Howard, Sr. and his friend, John Williams, owned this historic property, until almost one hundred years later, the Point was owned by descendants of those first colonial owners. Daniel Tolson became the eighth recorded owner of the Point when he purchased it from William Hatton Howard in 1855.

Twenty-seven years later, in 1882, E.D. and Clara Springer, from South Creek, North Carolina, bought the property and gave the Point the name by which it is known today. At that time one of the oldest houses on the island stood nestled among the oaks and cedars, protected from the frequent harsh winds that assailed the shoreline. Built by some of the earliest settlers, perhaps even by John Williams, the house, which included a prominent lookout tower, was rapidly deteriorating. The Springers used the house only occasionally, although they frequented the island almost every summer.

In 1923 the Springers sold their property to their son, Wallace. He was the last person to live in the old house, but only for a short while longer.

Wallace, who never married, remained on Ocracoke for some years. Instead of staying in the house, he eventually moved in with Mr. Jamie Styron and other island friends.

Older islanders remember exploring the abandoned house as children. It moved with the wind, and seemed to harbor unseen forces. Broken windows invited birds and other creatures inside. Wooden shingles had blown off the roof, allowing rain and moisture to break down and weaken joists and other timbers. Spider webs and bird droppings, combined with dust and mildew, infused the house with a sense of dread and foreboding.

Climbing the ancient staircase, young interlopers encountered ominous creaks and groans with each step. After dark, when shadows of gnarled and twisted tree limbs danced on walls, few islanders ventured inside the house. When they did, strange noises and mysteriously glowing lights greeted them. The short yelp or raucous squall of a close-by barred owl would send all but the most intrepid intruders scurrying to a more familiar place.

In 1941 Wallace sold the Point to Sam Jones, mainland Hyde County native and wealthy Norfolk businessman who had married into the Ocracoke Howard family. Wallace Springer died sometime after 1955.

By the time Sam Jones purchased the Point little was left of the house that was not badly in need of repair. Ocracokers remember not only the dilapidated old house, but also a smaller structure (a smokehouse or jail) with barred windows, as well as a long-abandoned stable.

When I was a small boy in the very early 1950s the house was nothing more than collapsed walls and piles of old lumber. Not long after World War II Sam Jones contracted with Mr. Walter O'Neal to dismantle the old dwelling. Mr. Walter used some of the lumber when building "Miss Dicie's" house on Howard Street. Other timbers were taken by Sam Jones for use as sills in his architectural masterpiece, Berkley Castle, and for a small house near Pamlico Sound for Eleanor Gaskins. People familiar with the Castle claim that five ghosts—two women and three men—wander the halls and rooms there. Could they be the spirits of the Williamses, or the Howards, or the Tolsons, or even some of the pirate crews?

House at Springer's Point

Sam Jones died September 27, 1977, and is buried at Springer's Point, next to his favorite horse, Ikey D. No remnant of any of the structures remains, with the exception of the base of an old brick cistern, now overgrown with ivy. Before the Land Trust purchased the Point, few people visited this area of the village anymore, especially after dark. Those who did often reported strange phenomena.

Roy Parsons was an accomplished island folk musician. In the 1930s Roy left Ocracoke to perform in the northeast, often playing at the Village Barn in New York City. After returning home he worked for Sam Jones for many years. For a while after Sam's death, Roy would visit his grave periodically to pay his respects. Years later, gesturing with his thumb and forefinger as if measuring a thick stack of banknotes, he told me, "If someone offered me a pile of one hundred dollar bills this thick to go down there to Springer's of an evening after dark, I'd tell him to keep his money."

On one occasion Roy was visiting Sam's grave just at dusk. He had run his skiff up onto the shore, and set his anchor on the beach. He walked toward the underbrush that leads into the protective enclosure that is Springer's Point. The sun was casting lengthy shadows as he approached. Once under the canopy of trees Roy could barely see to find the path. No sooner had his eyes adjusted when he noticed a figure sitting on the old brick cistern near the grave site.

"He was a big man," Roy explained. "He was wearing a black hat with a tall crown and a wide brim. He was sitting with his head down and his arms folded across his chest, and he was wearing a black silk waistcoat. His beard was long and gray."

Roy added that the sinister figure never raised his head, but he could tell he was following Roy's every movement.

"I turned around and started to walk back out," Roy explained. He felt a strange presence behind him, and he turned back to look. The figure was walking toward him, silently and deliberately. Roy turned around and began to walk faster. The figure matched Roy's pace. "By that time I was running," said Roy.

Roy ran back to his skiff as fast as he could, tripping over roots and branches, and scraping his arms and legs against the thick undergrowth. "I picked up that anchor and jumped right into my skiff," Roy explained. "I never even tried to pull that cord to start the motor. There weren't enough time. I just pushed off with my oar." Once out into the safety of the channel Roy ventured a look back.

He was just in time to see the figure moving out into the sound, the water up to his thighs.

And then the strangest thing happened. "He just disappeared. Went right on down like smoke," Roy related, obviously still spooked by his encounter.

Roy shook his head from side to side, raised his eyebrows and looked me straight in the eye. Roy was thin and frail, and his eyes bulged out of their sockets with an unexpected intensity. "I'm telling you," he said, pointing an arthritic finger in my face, "there's a difference between imagining something in your head and seeing it with your own eyes. I saw these things I'm telling you about just as surely as I see you right now."

Roy insisted that he would never go back down to Springer's Point again, especially after dark. "And," he continued, in an ominous tone, "you'd be wise to take my advice and stay away from there yourself."

(Readers who would like a more detailed history of Springer's Point are referred to Appendix II at the end of the book.)

THE MURDER OF
WILLIS WILLIAMS

WILLIAM Gaskill (1705/10–1770) was an early resident of Portsmouth Island, NC. William's eldest son, Benjamine (ca.1740–1787) married Jane Williams (d. 1801) of Ocracoke Island, NC. Their son, Jacob Gaskill, was born on Ocracoke in 1785.

Jacob was but two years old when his father died; sixteen when his mother died. At age 22, in 1807, he married Ann Scarborough. Together they had ten children. In 1827 Jacob was also appointed guardian of his wife's three nephews who were left orphans at the deaths of Ann's brother, George, and his wife Polly O'Neal. Five years later, in 1832, Ann died, leaving forty-seven year old Jacob with thirteen children to care for.

Jacob Gaskill, by all accounts, was an upstanding citizen. He was Ocracoke's Justice of the Peace, and seems to have been fairly well off. His large, two-story home, lathed in plaster, faced Pamlico Sound and sat on a large tract of land Down Point. In 1822 he sold, for $50, a three acre parcel of this land "for the purpose of enabling [the United States and their agent, Joshua Taylor] to construct and keep up a light house hereon."

Fifteen years later, five years after his wife died, and two days before his fifty-second birthday, on March 1, 1837, Jacob Gaskill was involved in an argument with his neighbor and first cousin, Willis Williams. It is said that Jacob went to talk with Willis on that fateful day, presumably in an official capacity as Justice of the Peace.

In an unrelated legal petition drafted two years earlier it is noted that whereas homes and businesses had, until then, been concentrated on the southern side of Cockle Creek, the "population of Ocracoke have greatly increased."

The petition points out that "where formerly [on the north side of Cockle Creek] there was no store, there is now three." These were T.S. Blackwell's store, John Pike's store, and Willis Williams' store and tavern (located near where the present-day Preservation Society Museum stands). The petition of 1835 indicates that there was some strife in the village and even mentions "evil disposed persons who are always ready to meddle with every persons business but there own."

Although neither Willis Williams nor Jacob Gaskill was named in the 1835 petition, it may be fair to assume that there were other rivalries in the village. In this case they may have been between the folks who lived on the northern side of the harbor (called creekers, and including Willis Williams), and those who lived on the southern side (called pointers, and including Jacob Gaskill).

So it seems that Willis and Jacob came to harsh words, possibly about property lines, rights of way, or some other land dispute. Or maybe the issue was related to Williams' tavern business. Perhaps he was selling alcohol to minors, or on the Sabbath. Local legend indicates that in the course of the argument Willis called Jacob a "god-damned son of a bitch."

Jacob turned away and started towards his home, "Don't be standing here when I come back," he is reported to have said. He retrieved his musket, and returned to find Willis exactly where they had been arguing. Willis was standing in the path, blocking passage. It was said he was holding his arms outstretched (perhaps as an act of defiance). That's when Jacob raised his musket to his shoulder, aimed, and shot his cousin in the left side of his neck. Willis Williams died instantly.

Ellen Marie Fulcher Cloud has researched this tragedy extensively. According to her, older members of the community had heard that Jacob and Willis were "fighting over a ditch which separated their property." But Ellen Marie could find no record of the two men ever having adjoining property.

Eventually Ellen Marie discovered an old map of Ocracoke which was part of the John Herritage Bryan collection. Mr. Bryan was a lawyer from New Bern, NC. The undated map, not drawn to scale, nevertheless gives clues to the murder of Willis Williams. Apparently entered as evidence in the trial of Jacob Gaskill, the map shows the home of "J. Gaskill." In addition to the three stores mentioned above, and homes (along with distances), the mapmaker drew in the footpath which ran from Jacob Gaskill's house to a footbridge across the "canal" joining the "Pond" (later known as Cockle Creek or Silver Lake.) to Pamlico Sound, and thence past Willis Williams' store and tavern to John Pike's store.

A figure is shown on the bridge, apparently facing south, in the direction of Jacob Gaskill's home. As Ellen Marie points out, the canal over which this bridge passes is the same narrow passageway used today by the state-run ferries and all other boats for access to Silver Lake. Today, as for generations of Ocracokers, it is known simply as the Ditch. The bridge has been long gone. It seems that the dispute took place on the bridge "over the ditch" on the path between Jacob Gaskill's home and Willis Williams' business.

Understandably, there seem to have been strong emotions surrounding the arrest and trial of Jacob Gaskill. Jacob, who pleaded "not guilty," believed that he could not obtain a fair trial in Carteret County, of which Ocracoke was at that time a part. The sheriff testified that the county jail was "insufficient for the safe keeping of the prisoner unless he be personally confined in irons" with a "suitable guard." This was done, and Jacob Gaskill was moved to the custody of the sheriff of Hyde County.

Interestingly, there is some speculation that Willis Williams, who had lived for a time on the mainland of Hyde County (and whose wife, Dorcas Credle, was from there), may have been involved in several disputes there. He also fathered at least one illegitimate child which may have contributed to further ill feelings. Jacob Gaskill probably knew that he stood a better chance of a lenient sentence in a jurisdiction that was known to look somewhat unfavorably on his victim.

In the spring of 1837, in Hyde County, Jacob Gaskill was tried and convicted of "felonious slaying," a charge similar to manslaughter. He was not found guilty of the more serious crime of murder. Nevertheless, as punishment he was branded on the palm of his hand with the letter "M." He suffered no other penalty, and immediately returned home to Ocracoke. In 1840 he is listed in the Ocracoke census, along with his children.

As an interesting side note, six months after the trial the steamboat *Home* wrecked on Ocracoke beach (see chapter 12). By that time John Pike was Justice of the Peace and Wreck Master (the person appointed by law to take charge of goods washed up on shore after a shipwreck). In a bitter dispute over their respective actions during rescue and salvage operations William Howard (grandson of the William Howard who purchased Ocracoke island in 1759) accused John Pike "through his influence and money" of rescuing "a murderer from the gallows merely for the sake of gain." Presumably this refers to John Pike's involvement in the murder trial of Jacob Gaskill. Other details of the murder and resulting disputes have been lost to history.

In 1845 Jacob married again, this time to Chloe Daniels of Wanchese, NC, and they had one daughter, Mary Frances, born in 1846. Jacob Gaskill is said to have kept his branded hand hidden for the rest of his life. He refused to shake hands. He also regularly gnawed at the "M" to erase the constant reminder of a deed he most likely rued until the day he died.

David Williams House/OPS Museum

In recent years the historic David Williams house was moved from its original location to the vicinity of Willis Williams' nineteenth century tavern. It serves today as the offices, museum, and gift shop for the Ocracoke Preservation Society. Staff at the museum report that not infrequently folks who walk by near dusk will glance up at the second floor windows and notice a man staring out from behind the parted lace curtains. Occasionally the figure will turn slowly to the side to reveal his neck, greatly disfigured as if mortally wounded by a gunshot. As quickly as it appears, the apparition vanishes.

FANNIE PEARL'S
DREAM OF DEATH

FANNIE Pearl MacWilliams was born September 13, 1894 Down Point. She was the daughter of John and Elizabeth MacWilliams. Mr. John MacWilliams owned and operated the "Department Store" on the south side of Cockle Creek Harbor. This was, by Ocracoke standards, a large conglomeration of buildings near the water that included retail stores and a dock. At the Department Store one could purchase groceries, clothing, shoes, hardware, chicken and horse feed, fishing supplies, housewares, and much more. The McWilliams family lived across the sandy lane, in a large Victorian house, within sight of the Ocracoke Lighthouse.

Lighthouse & McWilliams House

The Big Gut and the Little Gut, two languid tidal streams flowing from the harbor, through the village, then to the bald beach were still formidable barriers separating the Down Point and the Around Creek sides of the Ocracoke settlement. Hindered by still-primitive transportation and deep, sandy lanes, islanders only rarely ventured from one side of the village to the other.

When John and Elizabeth's daughter, Fannie Pearl, celebrated her seventh birthday the island's new Oddfellow's Lodge, constructed on a small parcel of land between the two guts, had just been completed. Fannie Pearl was one of the excited students to pass through the doorway when Ocracoke's first consolidated school opened its doors on the ground floor of the Lodge in 1901.

When Fannie Pearl was sixteen years old Ocracoke native Robert Stanley Wahab, who had left the island to obtain a higher education, returned to Ocracoke and was hired to teach the older students. He and Fannie Pearl gradually found themselves becoming attracted to each other. Stanley was only six years older than his beautiful and talented student, and in time they began courting.

In those days Ocracoke School offered classes only through the eighth grade. Fannie Pearl was a bright and capable scholar. Recognizing Fannie Pearl's aptitude and academic interests, her parents made arrangements to send her to boarding school on the mainland the next year for further education.

On learning that Fannie Pearl would be leaving the island, Stanley sought a teaching job in Norfolk, Virginia so he could be closer to his young sweetheart. The two lovers continued to see each other during the next school term, and were eventually married. They made their home in Tidewater Virginia. It wasn't long before Fannie Pearl discovered that she was pregnant. It was 1912 and she was eighteen years old.

In 1912 pregnant women were expected to sequester themselves until their baby was born.

Fannie Pearl decided to return to Ocracoke to rest and wait. She stayed Around Creek with Stanley's mother, Martha Ann Wahab, in her traditional white clapboard house with a deep, well-kept front lawn and white picket fence. Stanley remained in Norfolk to work. He regularly sent money home to his young wife.

One crisp October morning near the middle of her pregnancy Fannie Pearl greeted the sun with a disquieting sense of melancholy. She had had a disturbing dream during the night, and had tossed and turned for hours, unable to fall back asleep. At the breakfast table Martha Ann noticed Fannie Pearl's distant and somber demeanor, but was unable to learn the cause of her anxiety. As the day wore on Fannie Pearl felt the burden of her dream become more oppressive and she reluctantly agreed to share her mounting unease with her mother-in-law.

In her dream, Fannie Pearl explained, she had died. That was uncomfortable enough to recall. But in the surreal realm of dreams she had not only died, but her spirit had floated effortlessly above her own recumbent body and she could see that mourners had clothed her in a pure white funeral dress. She was lying motionless, eyelids weighted with silver coins, in a sparkling white casket lined in the finest smooth white silk.

Furthermore, her family had laid her casket gently across the gunwales of a sailing skiff that had been freshly painted a brilliant, spotless white. Sailing silently across the calmest and most serene of waters, through a star-studded night sky blacker than any she could remember, the white sailboat carried its charge to some distant and mysterious shore. Suddenly the silvery-white moon rose abruptly above the crowns of the ancient live oaks on the far horizon. The newly risen moon cast its unearthly glow upon the dark water and reflected from the heavy, white canvas sail. Silently and somberly the sailboat of death glided across the tranquil water.

Even after the telling Fannie Pearl continued to find the dream distressing, and it haunted her throughout the day. At sundown her angst intensified and she was reluctant to climb the steep, narrow stairway to her bed chamber in the attic. But she knew she must. Hours passed after snuffing out the candle on the night table beside her bed before she finally drifted off to sleep.

In the morning Martha Ann called Fannie Pearl downstairs for breakfast. There was no answer. Fearing the worst, Martha Ann climbed the stairs and cautiously opened her daughter-in-law's bedroom door. Fannie Pearl was lying lifeless under the handmade quilt on her feather bed.

Fannie Pearl had died during the night. Apparently her unborn baby had died *in utero* and the now lifeless child within not only drained Fannie Pearl's body of strength and vitality, but had slowly poisoned her bloodstream.

In 1912 Ocracoke had no telephones. Urgent messages were relayed by surfmen at the Life Saving Service via ship-to-shore radio. As soon as practical, after alerting neighbors and family of the terrible tragedy, Martha Ann walked silently to the station and asked the officer in charge to contact the station in Norfolk. They would relay her sad message to Stanley.

As soon as he received the terrible news Stanley sent back his reply. "Please," Stanley pleaded, "do not do anything until I can return home."

Immediately Stanley made plans to return to the island as quickly as possible. Before leaving Norfolk he arranged for a substitute teacher and enlisted friends and colleagues to help him get ready. Then he drove his flatbed truck to a funeral home and purchased their most beautiful casket. It wasn't that he disdained the homemade pine boxes local island carpenters made. But he did want the finest tribute he could provide for his young, deceased bride.

Early the next morning Stanley, still in shock from the dreaded news, left his home and drove to Atlantic, North Carolina. At noon Stanley was waiting quietly by the shore when the mail boat nudged up to the dock. There was a bustle of activity as passengers returning to the mainland from Ocracoke disembarked, and mail and freight were unloaded.

When almost everyone had left the dock Stanley knew what he must do. With help from the crew he reluctantly hoisted the gleaming casket onto the boat, then settled wearily onto one of the long wooden benches inside the passenger cabin. His heart was heavy, and his mind was numb as he tried to prepare himself for the four-hour journey across Pamlico Sound. He was content to keep to himself and resigned to little more than melancholy reflection. When the mail boat pulled up to the dock at home it was already late afternoon.

Martha Ann, along with family, close friends, and neighbors, greeted Stanley with the solemnity his reluctant return demanded. Stanley turned and walked the short distance down the sandy lane to his home, and stepped into the parlor to view the body and to mourn for his young wife and unborn child. Strong men had already carried the casket to the house, and they had laid Fannie Pearl's body gently inside.

In short order Stanley realized that his mother and other family and friends were beginning to be concerned. They had respected Stanley's wishes to wait for his return, but time was running out. In those days there was no way to embalm a body on the island, so most burials were made within 24 hours of death. Knowing that Stanley would not be home until that day, it was decided that no time could be wasted. The body was to be taken to the church for the funeral service, which was scheduled to begin immediately. Fannie Pearl's body must be interred as soon as possible.

Fannie Pearl had died Around Creek at Martha Ann's home, and that is where her body was. But her family cemetery was Down Point near her own family home. It was soon dark. And it was a long way following the Little Gut, out to the bald beach and back up the far side of the Big Gut, to the MacWilliams homeplace. The cart path was deep, soft sand in many places, and the trek would be time consuming and difficult.

The sensible solution was to lay the casket on a skiff and ferry Fannie Pearl's body across the Creek for burial that night. Boats were readied, one for the casket, others for the mourning party which had gathered along the shore. Soon they shoved off, and were on their way.

The freshly painted sailing skiff with the casket on board led the way. Rowboats filled with family and friends followed close behind.

Martha Ann was in the rowboat immediately behind the sailing skiff. The funeral procession was hushed and heavy-hearted.

Halfway across the Creek Martha Ann had time to reflect on the last several days. When she did, she noticed that the casket Stanley had purchased was not typical. This one was finished in a bright, gleaming white enamel. Within, Fannie Pearl, clothed in a pure white funeral dress, was reposing on a white silk pillow surrounded by the same smooth white silk lining. The casket was lying across the planks of a bright, freshly painted white sailboat with white canvas sails. The water was calm and the boat glided across the Creek with only gentle lapping as the bow cut through the surface. Martha Ann looked up. The night was dark and stars were strewn across the heavens like diamonds spilled from a jeweler's black velvet drawstring bag. And there, rising above the trees in the eastern sky, was a sight that took her breath away. It was the silvery white October moon illuminating the mournful procession.

To this day it is said that if you walk down by the harbor on the point side of Ocracoke village at nightfall, just as the full moon is rising, especially in the month of October, and stand quietly as you gaze out over the water, you can often hear what sounds like a woman's mournful gasp. Not a few islanders have suggested it is Martha Ann's gasp as she realizes that Fannie Pearl's "Dream of Death" came true that night so many years ago.

THE WRECK OF
THE STEAMBOAT HOME

I N October of 1837 the Steamboat *Home* wrecked on Ocracoke Island. It was the worst sea disaster ever to occur on Ocracoke. Ninety persons lost their lives that Monday night, October 9, as the 550-ton wooden, side-wheel steamer broke apart in the surf.

The *Home* was a 198 foot luxury vessel which, although it had made two previous voyages from New York City to Charleston, South Carolina, seems not to have been designed or constructed to endure the vicissitudes of the often unpredictable and violent weather in the North Atlantic, especially near the dreaded Cape Hatteras. This harsh lesson was learned only through unspeakable tragedy.

The *Home*, under the charge of Captain Carleton White, left New York harbor at four o'clock in the afternoon of Saturday, October 7, 1837, bound once again for Charleston. The *Home* was a grand and marvelous vessel. On her previous voyage she had exceeded all previously set speed records for travel between the two major ports. Excitement was palpable as the *Home* left the dock. One hundred and thirty persons, including forty crew members and ninety passengers, were aboard.

Virtually all of the passengers were well-to-do New Yorkers or Charlestonians. Their cabins were luxurious and their spirits high as they reveled in their finely appointed quarters and elegant surroundings, and looked forward to an enjoyable voyage.

Shortly after their departure, the *Home* ran aground on a shoal near Sandy Hook, New Jersey, and remained stranded for more than five hours. Finally, with the help of sails, steam power, and a rising tide, the *Home* was freed to continue her voyage. Now all hope of setting a new speed record was dashed.

The voyage continued for more than twenty-four hours without further delay, although the *Home* encountered increasingly stormy conditions late in the day of Sunday, October 8. By very early Monday morning gale force winds had intensified to hurricane velocity, and the *Home* was beginning to show alarming signs of distress. Captain White ordered the sails reefed. The storm grew wilder. The *Home* showed increasing indications of not being seaworthy.

By daybreak Monday morning crew members and passengers, including two veteran sea captains on board, had become so concerned that they called for the captain to beach the vessel as their only hope for survival. Captain White refused, explaining that the ship's owner, Mr. Allaire, had not insured the *Home*, and furthermore that his vessel was less than six months old, well built, and sturdy enough to withstand whatever torment the Atlantic could throw their way.

Soon after first light a leak was discovered, and one of the ship's boilers shut down. At that point Captain White turned the *Home* toward land, but headed back out to sea again when the boiler was returned to service.

The *Home* was now in the vicinity of Wimble Shoals, abreast of Cape Hatteras, and taking a harrowing drubbing from the worsening storm. Waves broke over the vessel, tearing off portions of the superstructure and smashing stateroom and dining room windows. The majestic wooden boat now creaked and groaned as it rode the heavy seas. Tiles began to fall from the dining room ceiling, and seawater was pouring in through seams in the ship's planking.

By 2 p.m. on Monday afternoon it was apparent that the ship's pumps were inadequate for dealing with the increasing volume of water the *Home* was taking on. Captain White pressed all aboard into service. Passengers and crew joined together on a brigade. Buckets, pails, pots, pans, derby hats, and other containers were put to use bailing the vessel, but by 8 p.m. the seawater had risen so deep that the *Home's* boilers were finally extinguished.

Now with only a few tattered sails, the *Home* was at the mercy of the raging sea. Captain White ordered his vessel turned to the west, toward the distant beach. It was his only hope. The *Home* had passed south of Cape Hatteras by this time and, although it was hours after sunset, the moon was waxing and the vessel was within sight of Ocracoke Island, about five and a half miles north of the settlement and the lighthouse.

Quickly filling with water, the *Home* limped toward the beach. Crew and passengers stood on the deck with dreaded anticipation. Finally, with a sickening thud, the steamer struck the outer bar, spun around, then listed onto her starboard side. The *Home* was more than one hundred yards from the shore and completely exposed to the thundering surf. Huge waves broke over the deck, tearing away the helm, the forecastle, lifeboats, and much of the rest of the super-structure in short order. Dozens of people were swept into the raging sea.

With great difficulty one of the remaining lifeboats was lowered over the lee side, but the angry breakers engulfed the small boat and it immediately capsized, spilling its occupants into the sea. No sooner was the lifeboat lost, than the mainmast crashed onto the deck, followed by the smokestacks. The *Home* was disintegrating rapidly. The starboard cabins and dining room were quickly demolished and the deck caved in soon afterwards. Within less than thirty minutes the *Home* was completely destroyed.

In the ensuing chaos every effort was made to protect the women and children, but eventually everyone was cast into the tempestuous sea. The vessel itself carried but one life ring. One gentleman had purchased a life vest before embarking, and he quickly buckled it on. Although he was temporarily knocked unconscious when his head struck a shattered piece of timber, he recovered and was washed onto the beach, alive and grateful.

Only forty people survived the wreck of the steamboat *Home*, including one twelve year old boy. All of the other children perished. The survivors found themselves, near midnight, cold, exhausted, and disoriented, on a desolate and unfamiliar beach. Seeing the light from the lighthouse, several men proceeded to walk the five miles to the village to seek help.

Bodies of the ninety victims of the greatest sea disaster in Ocracoke's history would later be found more than a mile from the wreck.

By daybreak the people of Ocracoke had heard of the terrible tragedy. They walked or rode their ponies to the site of the wreck to care for the survivors, and later to bury the dead and gather together any property that could be salvaged. Most of the dead were buried by the islanders in the nearby dunes in unmarked graves, many simply wrapped in sail canvas, blankets, or quilts.

After the disaster Captain John Salter, one of the passengers, who for a time seems to have acquired command of the *Home*, leveled charges against Captain White, accusing him of drunkenness and neglect, and claiming that the *Home* itself was not seaworthy. Ten other passengers joined him in his accusations. Whether the charges were true or false, Captain White was eventually exonerated.

As a consequence of the wreck of the *Home*, one year later Congress passed the first law requiring ocean going vessels to carry at least one life preserver for every person on board.

Stories of shipwrecks have been passed down on Ocracoke for generations. Island native Walter Howard penned the following tale more than fifty years ago. It was told to him by old Arcadia Williams, whose family was intimately involved with the aftermath of the steamboat *Home* tragedy. Walter's story is a brilliant account of the wreck and a fascinating glimpse into island life of more than one hundred and twenty years ago.

Walter Howard

The following version of Walter's story, *The Wreck of the Steamboat Home,* is abridged but the entire tale may be found on the Internet.

THE WRECK OF THE *STEAMBOAT HOME*, by Walter Howard:

When I was a small boy, I used to listen to the older people tell of the shipwrecks on Ocracoke Island where I was born. "God help the sailors on a night like this!" was, and is to this day, a household saying in our section of the country.

Old Arcadia Williams is responsible for the tale I'm about to tell. We will call her "Kade" as that was her nickname.

Kade lived in an old house framed from the beams of old shipwrecks. There were wooden windows and a wooden chimney which was always a source of wonder to me. Kade still did her cooking in the fireplace. The boys wanted to take up a collection to buy her a stove but she would have none of it. Her excuse was that old Ben Franklin was an infidel and that she would have none of his doings or inventions in her house.

Kade could "cuss like a sailor." Aside from this human weakness she was a good soul and didn't have an enemy in the world. As a story teller her equal has never been found.

She was a short, squat woman with a friendly, round face which boasted countless fine wrinkles. She parted her hair in the center and drew it into a tight knot terminating at the nape of her neck where she fastened it with two wire nails whose protruding heads gave the appearance that a carpenter had been trying to nail her head fast to her body without any marked success.

"It was in the fall of the year," she began, drawing the big cuspidor a little closer so as to get a better range for her spitting.

"It was in October, a heavy Northeaster had been blowing for two days and getting worse by the hour. It never blew any harder nor rained any more since Noah's Ark. Young'uns, I thought every gust of wind would be the last, as that old house of ours wasn't any too strong. It kept up for eight solid hours. The wind and rain was roaring so loud we could hardly hear each other talk. Along about two o'clock that night Father Jack had a nightmare. Young'uns, he almost scared all hands of us to death. Finally we brought him out of his fit and he told us his dream. He had dreamed of going down to the sea and beholding a terrible disaster with hundreds of people washed upon the sand, and he had picked up an infant only to discover it was drowned. As he stood there on the beach holding the child in his arms, the sea turned itself into a horrible monster and was reaching out with clutching hands trying to grasp him and pull him in with the rest of the drowned.

"While we were listening to this story there came a knocking at the door, and when brother Wid opened the door there stood as fine a figure of a drowned man as ever I laid eyes on. Before anyone had a chance to speak to him, he turned loose the door knob and pitched head foremost on the floor. It was fully a half hour before he was able to speak. He told us that he had just washed ashore from a steamer that had struck the beach about five miles away. Her name was the *Steamboat Home* bound from New York to Charleston with 130 people aboard. Upon reaching the beach he had groped around in the dark until he spied the light in our window.

"We drew our chairs up close to him and he told us his story."

"The weather was pleasant when we left New York on Saturday.

"The next morning a moderate breeze prevailed from the northeast. The sails were spread before the wind, and the speed of the boat was much accelerated. About noon the wind increased and the sea became rough. At sunset the wind blew heavily and continued to increase during the night. At daylight on Monday, it had become a gale.

"The sea raged frightfully from the violence of the gale, causing a general anxiety among the passengers. Early on Monday land was discovered, nearly ahead, which was believed to be the northern tip of Hatteras.

"The condition of the boat now was truly alarming—it bent and twisted when struck by the waves as if the next one would rend it asunder. The panels of the ceiling were falling from their places and the hull, as if united by hinges, was bending against the feet of the braces. Throughout the day the rolling and pitching were so great that no cooking could be done on board.

"Late in the afternoon the course was changed from southeasterly to north-westerly, when the awful truth burst upon us: the boat must be filling, for we could imagine no other cause for this sudden change. This was but a momentary suspense, for within a few minutes all the passengers were called on to bail in order to prevent the boat from sinking.

"Immediately all were employed, but with little effect, for notwithstanding the greatest exertions on the part of the passengers the water was rapidly increasing, and gave the most conclusive evidence that unless we reached the shore within a few hours, the boat must sink at sea.

"Soon after the boat was headed towards the land, the water had increased so much so as to reach the fire under the boilers and it was quickly extinguished. Gloomy indeed was the prospect before us, with 130 persons in a sinking boat far out at sea on a dark and tempestuous night, with no other dependence for reaching the shore than a few small and tattered sails; our condition might be considered tragic. But with all these disheartening circumstances, hope, delusive hope, still supported us.

"Although it was evident that we must soon sink, and our progress toward the land was slow, still we cherished the expectation that the boat would finally be run ashore and thus most of us be delivered from a watery grave.

"Early in the afternoon the ladies had been provided with strips of blanket that they might be lashed to such parts of the boat as could afford the greatest probability of safety.

"In this condition and with these expectations, we gradually, but with a motion nearly imperceptible, approached what to many of us was an unknown shore.

"At about eleven o'clock those that had been employed in bailing were compelled to leave the cabin as the boat had sunk until the deck was nearly level with the waters and it appeared too probable that all would soon be swallowed up by the foaming waves.

"Soon land was announced by those on the lookout. This, for a moment, aroused the sinking energies of all when a general bustle ensued, in the hasty, but trifling preparations that could be made for safety as soon as the boat should strike. But what were the feelings of an anxious multitude, when instead of land, a range of angry breakers was visible just ahead, and land was but half perceptible in the distance far beyond.

"Immediately before we struck, one or two passengers, aided by some of the seamen, attempted to seek safety in one of the boats at the quarter deck when a breaker struck it, swept it from the davits and carried with it a seaman who was instantly lost.

"A similar attempt was made to launch the long-boat from the upper deck by the chief mate. It was filled with several passengers and some of the crew but as we were already within the verge of the breakers, this boat shared the fate of the other, and all on board, about ten in number, perished.

"Now commenced the most heart-rending scene of all. Wives clinging to husbands, and children to parents, all awaiting the results of the next moment, which might bring with it either life or death. Though an intense feeling of anxiety must have filled every breast, not a shriek was heard.

"A slight agitation was, however, apparent in the general circle. Some few hurried from one part of the boat to another seeking a place of greater safety. Yet most remained quiet and calm observers of the scene before them. The boat, at length strikes—it stops—and is as motionless as a bar of lead. A momentary pause follows as if the angel of death shrunk from so dreadful a work of slaughter. But soon the work of destruction commenced. A breaker with a deafening crash swept over the boat carrying its unfortunate victims into the deep. At the same time a simultaneous rush was made towards the bow of the boat. The forward deck was covered. Another breaker came with irresistible force and all within its sweep disappeared. Our number was now frightfully reduced. The roaring of the waters, together with the dreadful crash of breaking timbers, surpassed the power of description.

"Some of the remaining passengers sought shelter from the encroaching dangers by retreating to the passage on the lee side of the boat as if to be as far as possible from the grasp of death.

"Already both decks were swept of everything that was on them. The dining cabin was entirely gone and everything belonging to the quarter deck was completely stripped away. All this was the work of about five minutes.

"The starboard wheelhouse, and everything about it, were soon entirely demolished. So much of the ceiling had fallen during the day that the waves soon found their way through all that remained to oppose them and were a few minutes time forcing deluges into the last retreat of those who had taken shelter in the passage already mentioned. Every wave made a frightful encroachment on our narrow limits and seemed to threaten us with immediate death. One lady begged earnestly for someone to save her.

"Another scene witnessed at this trying hour was still more painful. A little boy was pleading with his father to save him but the unhappy father was too deeply absorbed in the other charges that rested upon him even to notice the imploring child. For at that time his wife hung upon one arm and his daughter of seventeen upon the other. He had one daughter besides but whether she had been washed overboard at that time I am not certain.

"After remaining here some minutes the deck overhead was split open by the violence of the waves which allowed me an opportunity of climbing out. This I instantly did and assisted my wife through the same opening. As I had now left those below, I am unable to say how they were lost as that part of the boat was very soon completely destroyed, their further sufferings could not have been much more prolonged.

"We could see the encroachment of the devouring waves, every one of which reduced our thinned numbers and swept with it parts of our crumbling boat. For several hours previous, the gale had been sensibly abating. For a moment the pale moon broke through the dispersing clouds as if to witness this scene of terror and destruction and to show the horror-stricken victims the fate that awaited them.

"While the moon yet shone, three men were seen to rush from the middle to the stern of the boat. A wave came rushing on. It passed over the deck and only one of the three was left. He had barely time to reach a large timber to which he clung when this wave struck him—and he too was missing. As the wave passed away these men were seen above the water but they appeared to make no effort to swim. The probability is that the violence with which they were hurled into the sea disabled them. They sank to rise no more.

"During this time, Mr. Lovegreen of Charleston continued to ring the ship's bell which added to the gloom. It sounded like a funeral knell over the departed dead. Never before perhaps was a bell tolled at such a funeral as this.

"While in this situation our attention was arrested by the appearance of a lady climbing up on the outside of the boat. Her head was barely above the deck on which we stood and she was holding to it in a most perilous manner. She implored help. I ran to her aid but was unable to raise her to the deck. Mr. Woodburn of New York now came and with his assistance the lady was rescued. She was then lashed to a large piece of timber by the side of another lady.

"The former lady was washed ashore on this piece of wreckage beside me. I was compelled to get on a larger piece of the boat that lay near. This was almost immediately driven from its place into the breakers which instantly swept me from it and plunged me deep into the water. With some difficulty I gained the raft and continued to cling to this fragment as well as I could but was repeatedly washed from it, sometimes plunging deep into the water and coming up under it. After encountering all the difficulties that seemed possible to be borne, I was, at length, thrown on shore in an exhausted condition.

"At the time I was driven from the boat there were but few left. Of these, four washed ashore with me. On reaching the beach there was no appearance of inhabitants but after wandering some distance I saw your light and followed it."

"While this man was telling his story", Kade continued, "someone in my family sneaked out of the house and gave the alarm that a steamer was ashore.

"It wasn't very long before everybody knew about it and the whole population of the Island (about 300 people) turned out. Men began to run by with lanterns and torches, screaming 'Wreck on the Beach' and 'Vessel Ashore.'

"All the men folk went down to the wreck that night. As soon as the men arrived at the scene, they started to pull the drowned from the water. My father said that the last thing he found was a drowned child, the same as he had seen in his dream that very night. The following day was a sad day for this island as well as for the survivors. The menfolk had worked from four o'clock that morning until sundown. Every piece of canvas was used to sew up the dead in for burial, as well as all the bed quilts that were donated by the people here on the Island. Most of the dead could not be identified and were buried just as they had been washed ashore with their clothing and jewelry on.

"These earrings," Kade said, pointing to her ears, "were taken from the body of one of the ladies who had washed up on the beach. My mother had a complete outfit salvaged from an old trunk on the boat. It was the prettiest thing I had ever seen. The owner must have been a very wealthy lady. My mother never would wear it. She hung it upstairs where she could look at it now and then until it rotted away."

Having now finished her story, Kade fired one parting shot at the spittoon, toddled over to the window, looked out into the darkness and said in a voice almost inaudible, "God help the sailors on a night like this."

OLD QUAWK

THE story of Old Quawk (or Quork) has been told on Ocracoke Island since at least the early nineteenth century. In recent years many islanders have passed March 16 with hardly a thought for this colorful island character. Nevertheless, the basic outline of his story is well known.

In the late 1700s or early 1800s a man of indeterminate origin made his home on Ocracoke. Several miles north of the village, on a small hill, or hammock, he built his simple home of bulrushes and driftwood.

He had arrived on the island, some said, on a schooner from a distant land. Others claimed he had been shipwrecked on the beach and had decided to remain here. It was even rumored that he had once been a pirate. At any rate he was different from the other residents. Not only was he dark skinned (some think he was of African, West Indian, or perhaps Puerto Rican descent), by all accounts he was not a friendly sort of fellow. It is said he was often surly and disagreeable, preferring his solitude to interaction with the rest of the island community. When he became excited or argumentative people thought he squawked like a night heron. Hence the nickname, Old Quawk. No one seems to have known his given name.

Like the other men of the island, Old Quawk fished nets in Pamlico Sound. On March 16 many years ago (probably sometime in the early 1800s) the weather had turned nasty. Dark, menacing storm clouds had formed on the horizon, the wind had picked up and the sea was running rough. Thunder rolled across the Sound like ballast stones tossed about in the hold of a sailing ship. Lightning pierced the distant sky as if the Lord were coming back on Judgment Day. All of the island fishermen were concerned about their nets but more concerned still for their own safety. It was agreed among them that the day was much too stormy to risk venturing out in their small flat-bottomed sailing skiffs.

All agreed, save Old Quawk. His nets were too important to him and he had no fear. Cursing the weather, his weak-kneed neighbors and God himself, he set out in his small boat to salvage his catch and his equipment. He never returned, and he and his boat were never seen again.

For more than one hundred and fifty years seafarers from Ocracoke and surrounding areas paid healthy respect to the memory of Old Quawk by staying in port on March 16.

Old Quawk lives on in the names of landmarks near where he made his home: "Quawk Hammock" and "Quawk's Point Creek."

We may never know any more about Old Quawk. Roger L. Payne, in his 1985 book, *Place Names of the Outer Banks*, suggests that the name "Quawk" is actually a corruption of "Quake." During the colonial period, he informs us, coastal settlers often referred to marshy areas thick with certain grasses as "quaking hammocks." The grass would make a quaking sound as the wind rattled the close-packed spikelets. In fact, he says, there are even common references to "quaking bogs" in 14th and 15th century England.

Interestingly, Quacko (sometimes Kwaku, Quaco, Quack, Quock, or Quork) was also a relatively common African name retained by a few black slaves brought to North America in the colonial period who were not forced to adopt Anglicized names. Sometimes changed to Jacko or Jack, Quacko was often the name originally given to boys born on a Wednesday (some sources say Saturday).

Throughout the 1700s the name Quacko and its variants appeared sporadically in reference to slaves living in New York, Massachusetts, Virginia, and North Carolina.

In *The Waterman's Song, Slavery and Freedom in Maritime North Carolina*, David Cecelski relates that in the eighteenth century slave runaways and free black migrants were instrumental in forming a web of connection along the coast. "These distant ports [New Haven, Connecticut and New Bern, North Carolina]," he says, "were held together by black sailors such as Quacko, a slave who sailed out of Southport (then known as Smithville), North Carolina, who was said to be 'acquainted along the sea coast from New Brunswick [Georgia] to the Virginia line.'"

Could it be that all of these sound-alike names and words were conflated over time to bring us the tantalizing story of Old Quawk?

Maybe the very earliest settlers on Ocracoke did make reference to a particular quaking hammock about six miles north of the village. Not many years later a black sailor (a runaway slave, perhaps) could have found himself stranded on the island. In the early days of Ocracoke's history the isolated islands of the Outer

Banks were frequently lawless outposts. Home to shipwrecked sailors, pirates, and other hardy souls, a "live and let live" attitude often prevailed. Though not without their prejudices, settlers in maritime areas were often more likely than their inland counterparts to grant blacks a level of equality.

It would have been particularly easy for a black man to avoid trouble if he settled away from the village, in the vicinity of the quaking hammock, for instance. If his African name were the unfamiliar Quacko, and he spoke with a distinctive accent which reminded folks of the "quawk" of the local Black-crowned Night Heron, it would have been unremarkable that the quaking hammock would come to be remembered eponymously as Quawk* Hammock.

Perhaps Old Quawk was a better seaman than once imagined. Instead of being lost at sea in a raging storm, he might have found himself cast ashore days later near Southport, his modest camp on Ocracoke Island abandoned forever.

Stories sometimes fade, and superstitions pass with time. Nowadays many islanders do not even note the date of Old Quawk's battle with the forces of nature, let alone pay it any heed. But perhaps the time has come to invest this story with new life.

The next time you cross the bridge that leads across the creek that bears this colorful character's name, think of him on that fateful and tempestuous day, his angry fist raised to the heavens, cursing and inveighing against God and Mother Nature.

Perhaps you will even be a tad more cautious if you decide to go boating on March 16. Or maybe you will wait for another day, when the forecast is a bit brighter!

*On various older maps the hammock and creek are identified with the spelling Quark, Quoke, Kwawk, Kwak, Quork, or Quolk.

THE LEGACY OF THE
BLACK SQUALL

IN April of 1861 a square-rigged two-masted sailing ship, a brig, set sail from Havana, Cuba, bound for New York City. She was loaded with an unlikely combination of cargoes. The vessel carried a large quantity of sugar, a common but much sought after commodity in the nineteenth century. Along with the sugar was more unusual and quite exotic cargo, James Nixon's Royal Circus and Menagerie of Living Animals. On her nameplate the brig carried the colorful but disquieting name, *Black Squall*.

James Nixon (1820-1899) was a celebrated New York City showman of the middle and late nineteenth century. At the age of sixteen he secured a job as stable groom in Turner's Circus. He also worked as lamp trimmer, ring builder, and eventually as a performer. Nixon was enterprising, hard working, and talented. By the time he was in his twenties and thirties he had advanced to acrobat, then ringmaster, and eventually to equestrian director with a number of circuses performing in and around New York.

By 1857 Nixon had acquired sufficient capital to begin his career as an entrepreneur when he became co-proprietor of the Nixon and Kemp Circus. Within three years he was periodically associated with some of the greatest circus acts of the day, including Cooke's Equestrian Troupe, P.T. Barnum's Circus, and Grizzly Adams' California Menagerie. By 1860 he had ventured out on his own, and his newly assembled Nixon's Royal Circus was touring the southern states by rail.

James Nixon made a name for himself as an accomplished rider, and equestrian troupes constituted a central focus of his shows. In 1861 Nixon expanded his circuit to include Cuba. When the *Black Squall* wrecked at Ocracoke, Nixon's Circus had not only a troupe of trained horses and riders, but a sizeable collection of wild and exotic animals as well.

On April 8 the *Black Squall*, carrying Nixon's Royal Circus, encountered threatening weather off the coast of North Carolina. Inky thunderheads rose up in the southeast. The wind freshened and in short order gale force gusts whipped through the sails. The mercury in the ship's barometer fell to an alarming level. Jagged streaks of searing white lightning rent the sky, and thunder rattled across the deck. Waves broke over the bow and threatened to wash both crew and cargo overboard.

At the same time the tide was running high along the surf on Ocracoke Island. Islanders hunkered down around their fireplaces while rain pelted the roofs, and wind-driven rivulets ran down the window panes. Shutters banged against clapboards and every gust of wind found its way through cracks around windows and doors. Coal oil lamps flickered and cast ominous, dark shadows on bead board walls.

Massive live oaks groaned and creaked outside. Parents cringed with their children at the sounds of popping and cracking as limbs snapped and fell to the ground. The rising sea tide began to find its way across the tidal flats and into the village. Men stood by, armed with saws and hatchets, ready to scuttle their floors and let the tide in so it wouldn't float their houses off their foundations.

As so often happens along these treacherous shores, the captain and crew of the *Black Squall* were no match for the worsening storm. Out of control, and tossed about by the heaving seas, the *Black Squall* suddenly fetched up on the outer bar of Ocracoke's beach. There was no Life Saving Station on the Outer Banks in 1861 and little that islanders could have done to help, even if they had been aware that the brig was foundering offshore.

The relentless pounding of the breakers against the now stranded vessel took its toll. Most of the crew and passengers, including a young deckhand by the name of Jim Divine, managed to make it ashore as the brig broke apart. However, several people drowned that night, including two crewmen and William Nixon, a relative of James Nixon, as well as a young couple found on the beach locked in each other's arms. The young man was trim and muscular. Islanders assumed he was a leading acrobat with Nixon's Circus. The beautiful woman beside him, with long flowing blonde hair, was probably one of the talented riders who performed daredevil feats astride the trained horses.

The couple was bound together in a piece of sail cloth and buried on a nearby hill. Prior to burial an islander slipped a silver bracelet from the young woman's wrist. Inscribed inside were five simple words, "Till Death Do Us Part." The hill where they were buried became known as "Lover's Hill."

Passengers and crew were not the only losses on that terrible night in 1861.

Numerous casks of sugar on board were washed into the churning Atlantic Ocean.

As the *Black Squall* disintegrated in the angry surf, Nixon's animals were also cast into the water. What a sight it must have been! All manner of wild animals were washed up on Ocracoke's beach, including hippopotamuses, giraffes, and camels, as well as trained bears, tigers, and several lions. Many of the animals were drowned immediately, but several made it to the beach. Some collapsed and died, unable to go any farther. Others survived for weeks or longer.

Two of the horses were lucky enough to swim ashore safely. They were well-groomed Arabian steeds decked out in circus regalia. Their manes and tails had been plaited, and red silk ribbons tied onto them. Jim Divine stated that the mare was called Zero, and the stallion was named Nero. For years both horses roamed the island as they wished. Islanders were often amused and entertained as they walked the sandy lanes. If Nero or Zero happened to be nearby, the horses would dance, prance, and otherwise carry on, performing fancy circus tricks, hoping for an apple or other tasty handout. The bolder Nero was even known to wander into people's homes and eat from cast iron pots hanging in their fireplaces.

Jim Divine remained on Ocracoke for several months. He was on the island as portions of the wreckage were salvaged by islanders. Lumber was always sought after for houses, sheds, and outbuildings. Most of the sugar, however, was lost to the sea, and the circus paraphernalia was generally of little interest to the residents of Ocracoke. The colorful costumes were a curiosity, but no one except imaginative children had much use for them, although some were cut up and reused to make fancy bed quilts.

Parts of the large canvas tents were taken apart and made into serviceable sails for local fishermen, and no one objected when the preacher appropriated one intact tent for an impromptu revival. According to legend, the preacher started his sermon at Genesis, preached up to Revelation, and then continued back down to Genesis. He used the wreck of the *Black Squall* as inspiration for his sermon, explaining that human beings had no business corralling God's wild creatures and forcing the pitiful animals to perform demeaning tricks for sinful man's amusement.

Whether Jim Divine was one of the assembled listeners or not, we do not know, although it seems doubtful. He was young and experienced in the ways of the world. He was more likely to be found at a poker table or in a local tavern.

At one of the Saturday night square dances a pretty island lass by the name of Polly caught Jim Divine's eye, and the two were soon twirling about the dance floor. Polly was infatuated with this handsome young man as he entertained her with stories of distant ports he had visited and colorful characters he had met.

Polly's island beau, Bob Salter, was threatened by the developing relationship and promptly stepped up to the couple and whisked Polly away. Jim Divine followed and an argument erupted. Harsh words were spoken and the altercation quickly escalated. With tempers enflamed, a tragedy seemed inevitable. Lacking restraint, Jim Divine pulled a pistol from his pocket. In the blink of an eye a shot was fired and gun smoke filled the room. When the air cleared, Bob Salter lay dead at Polly's feet.

Immediately the young men who witnessed this crime of passion tackled the sailor and hauled him before the local magistrate, Mr. William Ballance. Emotions were running high, and Jim Divine was shackled and confined while the community dealt with their loss.

After the funeral a hasty trial was convened and Jim Divine was found guilty in spite of his protestations of self defense. Sentiments were strong against this recent intruder, although some witnesses agreed that Bob Salter had done much to provoke the unfortunate situation. Jim Divine was sentenced to be tarred and feathered and ridden on a rail through the village. His punishment began immediately.

Although his life was spared, Jim Divine was incensed by his treatment. Now an outcast in an inhospitable settlement on a remote island, he planned his revenge against the man who had sentenced him. William Ballance lived in a small cottage on the main thoroughfare (today referred to as Howard Street). Jim Divine, with weapon in hand, hid behind a large live oak tree across the lane and waited.

In due time William Ballance stepped outside to greet friends, and Jim Divine seized his opportunity. He raised his weapon, aimed, and squeezed the trigger. But the projectile missed its mark. Pandemonium ensued as Jim Divine fled the scene. A posse was soon formed and the village and surrounding woods scoured for the perpetrator. He was never apprehended. Islanders suspected that he swam out to a schooner anchored in the sound and escaped. Jim Divine was never seen or heard from again.

There was little left to remind residents of the *Black Squall*, except Nero and Zero. Some folks claim that Ocracoke's famous wild ponies are descendants of these two very fortunate survivors of the ill-fated brig. There may be some truth in this tale, but Nero and Zero were not the only horses to find their way to Ocracoke. Other shipwrecks, as well as early colonial settlers, had been instrumental in introducing horses to the island.

By 1883, when the United States government established the first Life Saving Station on the island, horses were being used to pull the beach carts laden with heavy life saving equipment to the site of shipwrecks. Captain James Howard, the Life Saving Service's first keeper, was especially fond of horses.

In the late 1800s, alarmed at the destruction of island vegetation because of the unfettered livestock, Captain Jim joined other concerned citizens in petitioning to have the free-grazing sheep, cattle, goats, and horses removed from Ocracoke. At the last minute, before sending the petition to the authorities, the keeper removed wild horses from the list. Although the wild horses contributed little to the problem that created the time of the blowing sand, and continued to be an invaluable resource for islanders for many years, some residents never completely forgave his deception.

Captain Jim had earlier purchased an Arabian horse from the mainland. His son, Homer Howard, broke and trained this horse they called "White Dandy." White Dandy was Captain Jim's pride and joy and was a constant companion to the keeper as he supervised the many rescue operations during the last years of the nineteenth century.

In addition to the central role they played in the U.S. Life Saving Service, their domestic use as beasts of burden and mounts for riders made ponies and horses a frequent part of island life.

For many years islanders held a roundup and pony penning on the Fourth of July. Young men would mount their steeds and ride to Hatteras Inlet the day before. In the morning they would locate the several herds and drive them together into the village.

In 1926 a squabble amongst the young island men threatened to cancel the annual pony penning. Captain Jim's grandson, Lawton Howard, and Lawton's best friend, Ansley O'Neal, both fifteen, decided that they were old enough to tackle this responsibility. They mounted their ponies on July 3 and rode to Hatteras Inlet (this was long before there were any paved roads on the island) where they camped out under the stars. Early the next morning the two boys began chasing the first small herd southward toward the village. As they encountered more horses they forced them to join the others. Occasionally some of the animals would swim out into Pamlico Sound and make the boys' job much more difficult. Finally, after a grueling day of hard riding in the blazing summertime sun, Lawton and Ansley rode proudly into the village behind several hundred stampeding Outer Banks ponies. It was a proud day for them both.

After the National Park Service purchased the majority of Ocracoke Island in the 1950s, the pony population was reduced to a more manageable size and eventually confined to a large penned area in the middle of the island.

Marvin Howard, one of Captain Jim's grandsons, was instrumental in building the first pony pen in the late 1950s. Captain Marvin was a native O'cocker who spent many years away from home sailing throughout the world, and then, in the early 1950s, retired back home to Ocracoke. He was well known on the island as a champion of young people and scoutmaster of the renowned mounted Boy Scout troop number 290. He wrote the following article, "Ocracoke Horsemen," which was reprinted in *The Story of Ocracoke Island*.

"Ocracoke Horsemen," by Captain Marvin Howard:

We hear a lot about the fishermen of the Outer Banks of North Carolina, but few stories deal with the equestrians of the Outer Banks. Surely some of them deserve to be proclaimed as among the world's best for their daring feats on horse-penning occasions. This is particularly true of the old days when as many as two-hundred ponies were penned on Ocracoke Island alone.

There have been wild horses roaming the Outer Banks since the landing of the Sir Walter Raleigh adventurers. None of these wild horses were ever large except the Pea Island pony which came from the original quarter-bred horse. (The quarter-bred horse, which has been developed as the finest cow-pony ever known, originally came from the Carolinas where they were bred for the quarter-mile race.) However, the ponies of the Outer Banks did vary in weight from five hundred to eight hundred pounds. They lived on the range the year round as wild as deer or wild horses can ever be. For sustenance they had only the salt grass, the boughs of live oak and red cedar, and when the winters were severe, they dug in the sand hills with their hoofs to get the succulent roots of the sea oats. These ponies no doubt had strains of Arab steed for in numbers of them there was untold beauty in color and build. They were fleet of feet, hardy, well lined, and full of muscle. They made fine saddle horses when properly trained. In recent times, two Ocracoke horsemen stand out. One was Homer Howard, the other was Monroe Bragg.

There are many people on Ocracoke who can recall their daring feats. People who have seen jockeys in America and England and have been to numerous horse-shows, carnivals, circuses, fat-stock shows, and rodeos in California, Texas and Mexico say that only on Ocracoke on the Outer Banks of North Carolina does the catching of wild horses with bare hands take place.

Captain Jim Howard was keeper of Hatteras Inlet Life Saving Station for a good many years. He owned quite a few cattle and wild ponies on Ocracoke. Jim bought a two-year old Arabian horse from somewhere on the mainland. His son, Homer Howard, broke and trained this horse for running the wild cattle and penning the wild ponies. His name was "White Dandy," though he was mottled with gray.

On "White Dandy" Homer on many occasions started at the north end of the island in the cool of the morning, driving the herd of wild ponies south. He rode merrily along across Tar-Hole Plains. There he would come upon a second herd of ponies headed by "Old Wildy," a long, rangy stallion. This herd, too, he would start driving southward. The third herd he encountered at Scraggly Cedars, then the Great Swash. After passing Great Swash he came to Knoll Cedars where the sheep pen used to be, and from there on southward the driving got touchy and more strenuous for the herds from the north were reluctant to go farther south and would try to cut through the thickets or sand hills back northward.

There were about two-hundred wild ponies in those days. They had to be driven over sand hills, through bogs, across creeks, through marshes, and through woodland thickets of myrtle, cedar, oak and yaupon. At about ten o'clock in the morning of pony-penning day, the horses could be seen spread out on the plains around "First Hammock Hills," just north of Ocracoke village. Each little band was headed by a tough and stringy stallion. They ran hither and thither, their manes and tails flying, heads held high, ears pointed forward, and necks arched to meet a foe. And whenever the stallions met, they did battle—biting, kicking, pawing—until the rider closed in. Then, they veered off from each other, returning to their herds. It was no easy task to drive these wild ponies sixteen miles southward to the corral in Ocracoke village.

Ocracoke boys perched in a big live oak tree with one limb at least thirty feet long to get the first view of the ponies as they were driven down the sandy road to Cockle Creek, the harbor. There were no docks in those days; the ponies were herded along the shore and in the shallow water to the corral by people on shore and in boats. After all the horses were penned and the bars closed, the people went home, ate dinner, and then returned for the branding and selling of the stock.

There were buyers from the mainland who wanted the ponies for saddle horses or for farm use. As soon as people began to climb the corral fence, a general movement among the stallions started. Hoofs began to fly, and teeth snap, with much squealing and snorting. Then, suddenly someone on the fence would yell "Homer's caught the motley roan over there."

To catch a wild stallion with nothing but bare hands took wit, agility, strength and stamina. Homer Howard would walk quietly through the mares, slapping them on the rump, working his way between them slowly, gradually—getting closer and closer to a great stallion—crouching panther-like, ready, alert—and in a flash he was astride the stallion, holding its mane with his left hand, throwing his elbow over the horse's withers, hooking his knee behind the elbow of the horse's front leg, reaching out with his right hand to catch the horse's lower face just above the nostrils, clamping down tight, and sticking there with the tenacity of a bulldog. The stallion would rear, pitch, squeal, snort, paw the air for thirty of forty minutes, but finally, out of wind, tired, and afraid, he stopped his violent struggling. Slowly the horseman eased his grip; immediately, the stallion lunged and reared. Only after several attempts did the horse admit his defeat. "Old Widdie," "Guthrie Sam," and "Rainbow" and others were truly great stallions and had the spunk and grit to put up terrible battles. Their tusks, or cutting teeth, were long from age and could be used to cut and slash, and their forefeet and rear hoofs held a wicked kick.

They used mostly McClellan saddles in those days, never western. Here again, Homer Howard was a master horseman, as he crawled astride and called for the blindfold to be snatched off. Then with a mighty heave the wild horse began to buck or run or sun-fish—backing, twisting, turning, rearing—coming to a full stop with head down, stiffened legs or standing on his hind feet, groaning in every nerve, his body sweat-soaked from his efforts, nostrils extended, expanding and contracting like a bellows. But finally he was out-mastered by the victorious horseman.

DIGGING UP
UNCLE EVANS

ALTHOUGH Ocracoke has retained much of its old world charm even into the twenty-first century, in many ways the island has changed significantly over the years. Some of the changes are the result of natural causes. Others are man-made.

George Howard Cemetery

More than eighty cemeteries scattered throughout the village bear silent testimony to the men, women, and children who shaped Ocracoke's destiny during the last three hundred years. Small family plots with traditional island names are nestled in woods beside narrow, winding footpaths...or in secluded yards behind weathered old homes...or in side yards under stately live oaks.

The inscriptions on the markers are familiar Ocracoke surnames—Styron, Garrish, Gaskill, Howard, O'Neal, Bragg, Williams, and a dozen or so others.

Unknown to many, bodies of other long-forgotten landowners, sea captains, mariners, pirates, and slaves lie buried under the shifting sands, many in unmarked graves.

In the eighteenth and early nineteenth centuries human activities contributed to a dramatic change in Ocracoke's topography. The first European owners of Ocracoke (in the early eighteenth century) did not live on the island, but used Ocracoke for raising livestock. By settling domestic animals on this remote and lonely island of sand, grass, and shrubs, they were able to protect their investment from predators, and at the same time keep them from wandering far astray. The ocean, sound, and inlets acted as natural fences.

Many years later, on a bitter cold night in January of 1923 Leevella Howard awoke suddenly about 3 o'clock in the morning. She sat upright in bed, eyes wide, and hands trembling. Her dream that night was eerily disturbing.

Leevella & Marvin Howard

Leevella's husband, Marvin Howard, was a sea captain. Marvin was as often at sea as he was at home. Understandably, Leevella worried regularly about his safety. More than a few Ocracoke fishermen and seafarers had lost their lives on the open water. In her dream Leevella saw Marvin walking slowly towards her. His manner was grim, his eyes fixed straight ahead. There was no smile or other expression on his face. Marvin wore his full dress uniform—captain's hat, dark blue jacket with brass buttons, starched white dress shirt, white gloves, neatly pressed slacks, and shoes polished to a luster. He clearly had a message for Leevella, but he said not a word. He simply walked towards her, slowly and deliberately.

Startled, Leevella awoke. She lay awake all night pondering the unspoken message. Had some terrible calamity befallen her beloved husband? At home on the island he regularly wore dungarees, a work shirt, no shoes, and a pith helmet he'd acquired in some distant land. Why, in her dream, was he wearing his captain's uniform? Marvin was generally jovial and he laughed easily. Why was his expression so melancholy? Why had he not spoken to her?

In 1923 there were no telephones on Ocracoke Island, and communication with the mainland was slow and sporadic. Leevella would only fully understand her dream days later when the daily mail boat pulled up to the dock in the late afternoon.

Marvin's younger brother, Evans, like so many islanders of the time, had left Ocracoke to work up north with the U.S. Army Corps of Engineers. Evans left in the summer of 1922, when he was only sixteen years old. He celebrated his seventeenth birthday on October 26 with his messmates on a dredge boat working the Delaware River in Pennsylvania and New Jersey.

On a quiet day in late January, 1923 Evans found himself spending time with several other young deckhands who, like himself, had been granted a day's leave. With few social contacts in the big city, they remained on board and amused themselves playing cards and chatting. After a midday dinner they made their way to the upper deck to enjoy the afternoon sunshine. As young men are wont to do they talked and joked and teased. Someone spied the ship's water hose and, as a prank, turned it on his companions. It was cold, but in no time at all the young men were running back and forth, hooting and hollering, and training the water hose on each other. In minutes they were all thoroughly soaked.

Evans, like his friends, returned to his bunk for clean, dry clothes. But he had difficulty getting warm. Even near the boilers he shivered and shook. He had been nursing a lingering cold. Now, with the exertion and dampness, his illness flared up anew.

Evans Howard

By nightfall his temperature had risen as his body attempted to ward off the invading germs. His immune system was compromised and he lay in his bunk for days, vainly fighting a raging fever and a worsening lung infection. He now had more than a common cold. He had developed pneumonia and was not recovering. In spite of the concerted efforts of his shipmates and a visiting physician, Evans died on January 21. He was just shy of seventeen years and three months old.

The responsibility to tend to Evans' burial fell on the shoulders of Marvin, whose vessel at that time was also docked in Philadelphia. Knowing what his parents would want, Marvin decided to take his brother home to Ocracoke. He had the body embalmed and placed in a simple wooden casket.

As soon as practical, Marvin made arrangements to accompany the body to Atlantic, North Carolina. There they placed Evans' casket onto the mail boat for the four hour journey across Pamlico Sound to his final resting place.

As a gesture of respect for his deceased younger brother, Marvin donned his dress uniform before embarking on the mail boat.

And so it was that Leevella understood her disquieting dream the moment Marvin, sad and grave, stepped onto the dock, steadying the casket with his white-gloved hand.

Zilphia & James Howard

The next day Evans was solemnly laid to rest in the small family cemetery on

Howard Street, near his grandparents, James and Zilphia, and various uncles and aunts. There he remained for nearly a quarter of a century.

On May 15, 1947, Evans' father, Homer Howard, died, and was buried in a newly laid out graveyard several hundred feet down the lane. Not long after Homer's interment, his wife, Aliph, became distressed that her son, Evans, was not buried near his father.

Ocracokers were accustomed to taking matters into their own hands, and this was no exception. In the mid-twentieth century isolated Ocracoke Island was, for all practical purposes, immune to many of the laws of the state.

After careful consideration Aliph spoke with my father, Lawton Howard, Evans' younger brother, and asked him to exhume and relocate his brother's body.

With shovels in hand my father and mother, accompanied by my older brother and me, walked to the graveyard and began their cheerless task. I was three years old. The sand yielded easily to my parents' spades, and directly they spied a tarnished brass handle. The wooden casket had long since deteriorated. Fractured pieces of rotted wood and the six brass handles soon lay on the ground along with a small plaque engraved with the words, "Evans Howard, 1905—1923."

They easily retrieved the larger bones. Skull, ribs, pelvis, femurs…my parents carefully extracted them from the grave and laid them gently in a peach basket. Within the hour they had nearly filled the basket.

Towards the end the task became more difficult. As my parents searched the ever deepening hole for more bones the smaller ones slipped through their fingers and were covered with sand as the sides of the grave began to deteriorate. Try as they might, the smallest finger and toe bones eluded their grasps. Unwilling to give up, my parents lowered me into the grave, but I was only moderately successful in collecting more of Uncle Evans.

Finally my parents abandoned their search, pulled me up, and reluctantly filled in the grave. They carried the basket down the lane and quietly reburied Evans' bones next to Homer, just as Aliph had requested.

For as long as I can remember I had heard this and numerous other intriguing and fascinating stories of Ocracoke and her unconventional ways. But it wasn't until I was nearly sixty years old that I understood the origins of my nightmare about the skeleton chasing me.

In my dream Howard Street morphs into the bald beach. The dreadful skeleton chases me across lonely tidal flats, a barren wasteland where the Bragg family burying grounds were located during the time of the blowing sand.

The skeleton who fixes me in his gaze and lunges at me rises from a wind-swept grave and is always missing his small finger bones, just as Evans is missing his to this day.

Homer & Aliph Howard House

More than eighty years after Uncle Evans' death I embarked on the rehabilitation of my grandparents' 1865 home, just a stone's throw from our Howard Street cemeteries.

As we prepared the 140 year old bead board walls for painting we discovered a curious marking in an upstairs bedroom. On the wall in the corner we noticed a faint pencil inscription. I had never seen it before, nor had anyone else. On close inspection the words came into view, "Evans Howard."

Could Uncle Evans be sending me a cryptic message from beyond the grave?

We painted the walls white, but left that small corner, between the window and the rear wall, uncovered, a reminder of Uncle Evans and his graveyard plight. The dreams have stopped. No longer does the skeleton without its finger bones menace me in my sleep. I even sleep in the same room with Uncle Evans' signature on the wall.

Folks will tell you that they walk warily along Howard Street after dark. If you venture there you will not want to linger, especially along that lonely stretch between where Evans Howard (or at least most of him) lies, and where his finger bones lie. More than one person has reported seeing a vague figure, a ghostly skeleton, wandering deliberately back and forth among the gnarled live oaks, yaupon bushes, and ancient grave markers. He rarely gives chase; he simply walks, slowly and deliberately, hoping perhaps that someday his bones will be reunited.

Appendix I

Principal Characters

- Blount, Winnie (ca. 1836—ca. 1920) & Harkus (ca. 1819—ca. 1890), progenitors of Ocracoke's only post-Civil War native black family
- Foster, Bunia (1888—1928), island native whose death was accompanied by an unusual omen
- Howard, Evans (1905—1923), the author's uncle, buried in two places on Howard Street
- Howard, Homer (1868—1947) & Aliph (1876—1950), Coast Guard surfman and his wife; grandparents of the author
- Howard, James (1838—1904) & Zilphia (1841—1919), first keeper of the Cedar Hammock Life Saving Station (1883—1903) and great-great-grandson of William Howard, Sr.; and his wife
- Howard, Marvin (1897—1969) & Leevella (1898—1982), sea captain, author's uncle, and founder of the Ocracoke mounted Boy Scout Troop; and his wife
- Howard, William, Sr. (< 1700—ca. 1795), last colonial owner of Ocracoke Island (July, 1759), alleged quartermaster to Blackbeard the pirate, and great-great-great-great-great-grandfather of the author
- Howard, Walter (ca. 1897—ca. 1959), native island musician and locally celebrated raconteur
- Garrish, James Henry (1877—1947), island native and first owner of a house that some claim is haunted
- Gaskill, Jacob (1785—ca. 1865), Ocracoke Justice of the Peace and principal in Ocracoke's first murder

- Godfrey, Mr. & Mrs. (early—mid-twentieth century), island innkeepers and principal characters in an island mystery and ghost tale
- Jones, Sam (1893—1977), wealthy Norfolk businessman and eccentric part-time islander
- Old Quawk (late 1700s, early 1800s), surly castaway sailor who made Ocracoke his adopted home
- Parsons, Roy (1921—2007), native islander, musician, model boat builder, and storyteller
- Rondthaler, Theodore (1899—1966) & Alice (1899—1977), Ocracoke School principal and teacher; and his wife, also a teacher
- Scarborough, Charlie (1874—1958) & Sue (1878—1954), island carpenter and his wife
- Springer, E.D. (1838—1925) & Clara (ca. 1840—1923), mainland North Carolinians and one-time owners of Springer's Point
- Thomas, Capt. William (1857—1930) & Eliza (1866—1946), North Carolina sea captain and his wife
- Tolson, Daniel (1816—1879), island native and early owner of Springer's Point
- Wahab, Fannie Pearl McWilliams (1894—1912), island native and first wife of Robert Stanley Wahab
- Wahab, Robert Stanley (1888—1967), teacher, businessman, and early promoter of Ocracoke Island
- Williams, Arcadia (1842—ca. 1899), colorful island storyteller and great-granddaughter of John Williams
- Williams, John (ca. 1725—1787), friend of William Howard and purchaser of one half of Ocracoke Island in September, 1759
- Williams, Willis (ca. 1800—1837), murdered island tavern owner and first cousin to Jacob Gaskill

Appendix II

More About Schoolhouses

THE first recorded island school master was Henry Garrish, who was hired in 1785 by the estate of Jobe Wahab for 4 pounds, 16 shillings to instruct his young son, Thomas Wahab.

Undoubtedly this was a private venture. At that time only a select few of Ocracoke's residents were literate, and the community was unable to support free public education.

Mention of a schoolhouse occurs in the very early nineteenth century. It was then that William Howard, III. [sometimes referred to as William Howard, Jr., and later, after the death of his father, as William Howard, Sr.] sold a parcel of land to the "subscribers of the schoolhouse." In the deed, dated February 4, 1808, William Howard sold "a certain parcell of land lying where the schoolhouse now stans…" We can only guess when this building was erected and where, exactly, it stood. We may presume that William Howard had earlier leased this property to the school subscribers, or at least given his permission for a schoolhouse to be built there.

We do know that William Howard's land lay on the north side of Cockle Creek. Local tradition indicates that an early schoolhouse was situated in the vicinity of the present-day firehouse, probably directly across the street. This tract is included in the historic Howard family property.

In the 1808 deed William Howard also grants the subscribers of the school-house the "priviledge of giting wood for the benefit of sd [said] School house as far as get enuff for the use of the house of any kind except live oak and cedar…" Presumably he was granting the privilege of cutting firewood on the remainder of his property.

One year later, in 1809, Edmond Dailey, one of the witnesses to the 1808 deed, rented land from John Williams. Early in the twentieth century it was said that John Williams' shell pile could still be seen near where the Thurston House Bed and Breakfast now sits. This land borders property owned by William Howard in the early 1800s. The rental agreement, which states that Edmond Dailey would have a house, pig pen, and fig orchard, also mentions that Dailey was a school master.

Sometime around 1825 Ocracoke residents joined together to finance a new schoolhouse. Approximately $500 was raised from at least 27 individuals in amounts ranging from five dollars to twenty-five dollars. A formal document was drafted specifying their goals and outlining the rights and responsibilities of the school subscribers. The first regulation stipulated that "a piece of land shall be purchased of at least the one half of an acre some where on or near the main road leading from the dwelling of the late William Williams, to that of Thomas O'Neal."

The "main road" at that time went from the Point [Springer's Point], in front of the newly constructed lighthouse, past the present-day Methodist Church and schoolhouse, near the present-day firehouse, and thence to a ridge close to the north sound shore, and perhaps from there all the way to Hatteras Inlet. Thomas O'Neal owned land in the vicinity of today's firehouse. Perhaps this new schoolhouse was the one built across the street from the present day firehouse. And maybe it was not far from the original schoolhouse that was mentioned in 1808.

The "Union School House" document, as it was called, indicated that this new building was also slated to be used for church services when school was not in session.

The first mention of a church on Ocracoke is in 1828. Presumably it was this congregation that made its home in the newly built schoolhouse. In fact, a crude map of the village, part of a legal petition dated 1835, identifies one structure as the neighborhood church. No schoolhouse is indicated, though we may presume these were one and the same.

No one knows what happened to this early building. The area where it was located is known to be low and susceptible to flooding during high tides. The schoolhouse may have been destroyed by a storm or hurricane many years ago. Eventually the land was abandoned. In later years another islander "took up" the land, as Ocracokers say, for the payment of back taxes.

Local tradition also indicates that an early school was established for the benefit of the children of men serving in the Life Saving Service. In certain documents this is referred to as "Captain Wilson's School." It seems reasonable to assume that this school operated at Cedar Hammock, near Hatteras Inlet, during the late 1800s when the Life Saving Station there was active. No one seems to know any further details.

Sometime before the Civil War, Ocracoke was served by at least two schools. A document dated November 2, 1868 states that the existing schoolhouses were destroyed during the war. The document, signed by John S. McWilliams and A.B. Howard, does not specify whether the buildings were destroyed because of the war or because of some other factor (fire or storm?) during that period. It points out that two schoolhouses were now required. Presumably this was to best serve residents on both sides of the village. The document also says that one "Select School" opened that very day with twelve pupils, at a fee of "one Dollar per Lunar month."

We know that Sarah Owens Gaskill ran a small private school in the vicinity of Clinton Gaskill's home, under the shadow of the Ocracoke Lighthouse. Sarah E. Owens was born in 1840, only 17 years after the 77 foot white tower was erected. She hailed from Washington, NC and moved to Ocracoke when she married island native, Benjamin Decator Gaskill, Sr.

Sarah Owens Gaskill's school may have been the Select School mentioned above. Island tradition suggests that she operated her private school for quite a few years in the latter half of the nineteenth century. She died in 1915.

Sarah Owens came from a sophisticated family. She was a cousin to Susan Dimmock (1847-1875), the first female surgeon in North Carolina. Susan Dimmock's family had moved to Washington, NC from one of the northern states after her father purchased a newspaper in that city. When her father died at the onset of the Civil War, Susan and her mother moved to Boston.

In 1867 Dimmock, then a student at the New England Hospital for Women and Children in Boston, and another woman, Sophia Jex-Blake, applied for admission to Harvard and were turned down by a vote of seven to one by the faculty. Following another attempt to gain admission to Harvard the next year the medical staff stated, "this faculty do not approve the admission of any female to the lectures of any professor."

Because no United States schools would accept a woman in their surgical programs Dimmock looked to Europe. She applied to and was accepted at the

University of Zurich Medical School. After completing her studies she returned to the United States to practice medicine. In 1872 she was accepted into the Massachusetts State Medical Society. Three years later, at only twenty-eight years old, Susan Dimmock was drowned in the North Atlantic when the ship on which she was a passenger struck an iceberg and sank.

Although not a resident of Ocracoke, Susan Dimmock's legacy carried over to islanders. Her story has been retold for generations, and several island children have been named for her.

Also in the late 1800s a Mr. Manson from Beaufort, NC taught at a private school located in the home that later was owned by Wheeler and Tressie O'Neal Howard, on the corner of Howard Street and School Road. The old house was torn down in 1970, and a new one built on the same lot. Mr. Manson was from an aristocratic family in eastern North Carolina. He was active in the community, was an accomplished musician, and played the organ in the Methodist Church. He lived on the island and operated his school for only two or three years.

On August 15, 1881 Ocracoke residents again petitioned the state for two schools. Thirteen years later, in 1894, James M. Bragg and his wife, Laurette Bragg, sold to the school committee a parcel of land Down Point for a school-house. Tradition suggests that the schoolhouse was already on the land, however, moved by the "hand of God."

In the late 1800s a fierce storm brought tide into the village from the ocean side. The school building Down Point was badly damaged. Accounts indicate that the sea tide swirled around the building and undermined the foundation piers. As the tide rose higher the schoolhouse was lifted up and washed across the road onto a lot where Leroy O'Neal now has a home, not far from Albert Styron's store. Presumably this was the land that the Braggs sold. Since the schoolhouse was now sitting on the land, it seemed only prudent to sell that parcel to the school committee. This building continued to be used for a while afterwards, but it was eventually demolished.

In a letter dated June 29, 1895 island store owner, Michael Lawrence Piland speaks about "the present schoolhouse" in reference to land about to be purchased for a new school on the creek (or north) side of the village. He states that the existing schoolhouse "is in just as good condition as it has been in for the last ten years…" and challenges the decision to purchase land for a new building.

Nevertheless, in July of 1898 Benjamin F. Williams and his wife, Mary G. Williams, sold one quarter of an acre of land ("a part of the Toler Land") to the "Public School Committee," whose members were W.E. Howard, J.W. McWilliams, W.H. Tolson, H.F. Jackson and E. O'Neal. No new schoolhouse appears to have been built there. It seems that the older schoolhouse was located in the vicinity of Iona Teeter's present-day home on the British Cemetery Road, and continued to be used for several more years. Older island residents remember hearing tales from their parents indicating that the schoolchildren played under a large live oak tree "behind John O'Neal's house." The oak, unfortunately, was cut down when the British Cemetery Road was widened and paved in the late 1950s.

Some remember that the schoolhouse sat where the road is now. It is said that the building was perched on a tussock and that the school children could jump out of the windows directly into the path that passed between the large oak and Chris Gaskill's home.

As mentioned earlier, in 1901 Ocracoke Lodge No. 194 Independent Order of Odd Fellows built a two story wood frame building to serve as their lodge. The lodge, now the center section of the Island Inn, sat between the Big Gut and the Little Gut. Soon after its construction both island schools were abandoned and consolidated, and public school was held on the first floor. In February of 1911 Benjamin Gaskill O'Neal was paid $3.74 for taking a census of children on Ocracoke. He recorded 187 children of "white race."

At that time island native Miss Laura Tolson was also operating a private school Down Point. Laura Tolson was born May 10, 1861 in the house later owned by Theodore and Alice Rondthaler. She taught school there as a young woman. After Laura Tolson's mother died and her father remarried, Laura and her sister, Malsey Jane, moved in with their uncle, Daniel Tolson, who lived at Springer's Point.

When Laura's Uncle Dan Tolson died in 1879 she went to live with her sister who had by then married Robert Gaskill. They had recently purchased a small house Around Creek from Enoch Ellis Howard. This house, in the 1950s the home of Murray and Elsie Tolson, is now a rental cottage behind the Island Ragpicker gift shop.

Not long thereafter Laura fell in love with the young and handsome Methodist preacher, J.C. Smith. By all accounts he was a bit "peculiar" and Laura's family tried to dissuade her from marrying him. As often happens, she did not heed their advice. Not long after the nuptials Rev. Smith had a major breakdown and his family came to the island to take him home. Eventually he was committed to an institution. Laura and Rev. Smith never lived together again, and she never remarried.

Laura Smith's school was located in a small building constructed in her sister and brother-in-law's yard. Local tradition indicates that she operated her school for quite a number of years, although she also taught at the public school held at the Lodge. After her sister died in 1915 Laura declined to stay with her brother-in-law, and moved Down Point to live with her brother, Daniel Tolson, "so people wouldn't talk." She died in 1934.

Ocracoke School, 1917

In 1917 a new schoolhouse was built near the home of Calvin and Iva O'Neal. This attractive new building, with six rooms, each with its own entrance to the outside, housed grades one through eight, and soon became a focal point for the community. In 1928 Beulah O'Neal and Fannie Pearl Fulcher earned $75.00 per month as teachers. In 1929 principal Joseph Hamilton was paid $119.35 per month, while teachers Carrie M. Williams and Beulah O'Neal earned $50.05 and $61.60 respectively.

Island children who wanted a high school diploma were forced to leave the island. Most of these attended boarding schools in eastern North Carolina.

Class of 1931

Eventually Ocracoke School added a high school program. The first graduating class was in 1931 when Russell Williams, Mable Fulcher, and Lucy Garrish finished the eleventh grade (the highest grade available at the time). Their principal was David Taylor.

In 1952, under the direction of the Rondthalers, substantial improvements were made to the Ocracoke School with the help of state funds. Asbestos shingles were put on the roof, electric lights were installed, indoor plumbing was added, and a new steam-heating unit replaced the old pot-bellied stove.

This schoolhouse served the community well for over half a century. By 1970 the community decided to tear down the old schoolhouse and build a new one in its place. There was by no means universal agreement on this decision. Many residents expressed regrets not only because the 1917 building was aesthetically pleasing, but because it was constructed of sturdy heart pine that many thought far superior to wood available in the 1970s.

Students attended classes in the Methodist Church Sunday School rooms during the razing of the old building and the construction of the new one. The new schoolhouse was completed in the summer of 1971. In 1977 a gymnasium, additional classrooms, and a shop were added. In 2006 a new two story addition provided much needed extra classroom space.

APPENDIX III

MORE ABOUT SPRINGER'S POINT

WILLIAM Howard, Sr. purchased Ocracoke Island on July 13, 1759. He was the last person to own the entire island, and the first of the colonial owners to make his residence there. Less than two months later, on September 26, 1759, William Howard sold one half of the island to his friend, John Williams.

John Williams' portion of Ocracoke included what is now known as Springer's Point. In June of 1787 Williams sold a sizeable section of his holdings, including the Point, to his son, William Williams. William Williams (born 1745/50) died intestate in 1799. At the time of his death he owned land extending from the mouth of Cockle Creek (the Creek is now known as Silver Lake; the mouth is called the Ditch), around the western edge of the Creek, and from there, south, all the way to the ocean and around the sound shore, back to the Ditch.

During this period of Ocracoke's early history the north shore of Ocracoke Inlet was much closer to Ocracoke village and to an area referred to today as the First Grass. It was only later, after William Williams purchased the land from his father, that the South Point built out to frame the present-day inlet.

In 1801 William Williams' holdings were divided among his heirs by court-appointees. Six plats were designated, one each going to the following:

- Comfort Williams, daughter (and her husband, George Dixon from Portsmouth Island)
- Elizabeth Williams, daughter
- William Williams, son
- Delancy Williams, minor daughter

- Thomas Wahab, guardian to Delancy Williams
- The public pilots (Six and one half acres of Comfort Williams' portion was conveyed for the use of these pilots. This was set aside to compensate for the loss of other public land due to erosion.)

As mentioned, many of the earliest permanent settlements in Ocracoke village were situated on the southwest side of Cockle Creek (Silver Lake). According to a legal petition and map from 1835 only one public road had by then been laid out on Ocracoke Island. It began at the sound (near Springer's Point), went by the lighthouse (built in 1823), then continued past where the present-day Methodist Church and school are situated. From there it passed the original Methodist Church (which was established in 1828, and was located near the present day firehouse), to a ridge some distance away, and then to the north end of the island. The petition averred that this one road, from its establishment until 1835, had "served the purpose of all the inhabitants" of the village of Ocracoke.

In 1814 William Howard, grandson of the first William Howard, acquired land and, in 1820, a house, in a part of the village known then simply as the Point. He purchased his two-story "dwelling house," along with a storehouse, from Mary Cabarrus who acquired the buildings from her uncle, Augustus Cabarrus, one of the early pilots. Interestingly, these individuals owned only the structures but not the land, as this six and one half acres was an expansion of Pilot Town and was set aside for public use.

Another deed from July 23, 1820 indicates that William Howard purchased one half of an additional storehouse and lot adjoining the public lands.

By 1832 William Howard was ready to sell part of his real estate to his son-in-law, Elisha Chase. Chase was a New England sea captain who had married William Howard's daughter, Thurza, in 1821. Nineteenth century Customs Records indicate that William Howard and Elisha Chase were co-owners and masters of several schooners in the 1830s.

According to a deed dated May 15, 1832, William Howard sold Chase one half of a piece of land which he had purchased from Comfort Dixon on January 15, 1831.

Although the description of this parcel of land is somewhat unclear, it definitely includes the area of large live oaks commonly known today as Springer's Point. William Howard mentions several buildings on his property including "two old kitchens," a "smoke house," a "new kitchen" an "old store house," a "wharf," a "new warehouse," a "store," two other "houses," a "blacksmith shop," and even a "windmill," as well as his own home, which he describes as "two dwellings attached together." All of these, he says, "are now, and have long been the property of the said William Howard." At least some of these structures appear to have been built on the six and one half acres of Pilot Town, which was not private property.

William Howard's dwelling place was the two-story house purchased from Mary Cabarrus in 1820. This house, as previously mentioned, was actually two houses joined together. Constructed sometime before 1800, part of it may have been built by John Williams or his immediate heirs. Legend suggests that this building may have originally belonged to Edward Teach, although this is highly unlikely. The pirate captain probably had nothing more than a temporary campsite on Ocracoke Island.

Sometime before 1850 Elisha Chase sold his island property back to his father-in-law, forsook the life of a sailor, left Ocracoke, and led his family west with a wagon train. Near the end of their journey both Elisha and Thurza fell seriously ill. Thurza died and was buried along the trail in Tennessee. Elisha, with his three children, William Howard, George Howard, and Thurza, eventually settled in Missouri.

At William Howard's death on August 30, 1851, his son, William Hatton Howard, inherited a sizeable portion of his father's property, including the tract that had been called Williams' Point, and more recently, Howard's Point. Four years later, in 1855, he sold his inheritance to Daniel Tolson who immediately made his home on the Point. William Hatton moved to Florida where he died after being thrown from a runaway carriage.

A conspicuous feature of the house at the Point was an observation tower that rose above the tops of the trees. This tower was a later addition, possibly built by Daniel Tolson, and from there the occupants of the house had a commanding view of the Atlantic Ocean and Pamlico Sound. Any ships approaching Ocracoke Island would have been easily spotted by a lookout in this tower. If pirates had ever inhabited this dwelling their spirits would have welcomed the addition of the tower.

After Daniel Tolson's death, his wife, Sidney, inherited the property and then married John Small McWilliams. One year after her death in 1882 the Point was conveyed to E. D. and Clara Springer, of South Creek, North Carolina. Although the Springers enjoyed spending time on Ocracoke they never made this their permanent home. Eventually the Springers' son, Wallace, acquired the Point. In 1941 he sold his Ocracoke holdings to Sam Jones. After Sam's death in 1977, his heirs sold the property to private developers. They, in turn, conveyed the majority of Springer's Point to the North Carolina Coastal Land Trust for use as a nature preserve.

APPENDIX IV

THE AUTHOR'S GENEALOGY

William Howard, Sr.
Blackbeard's Quartermaster, Owner of Ocracoke Island
(ca. 1686—ca. 1794)
⇩

William Howard, II
(ca. 1745—ca. 1795)
⇩

William Howard, III
(ca. 1765—ca. 1823)
⇩

Solomon Howard
(1807—1853)
⇩

James Howard
(1838—1904)
⇩

Homer Howard
(1868—1947)
⇩

Lawton Howard
(1911—2002)
⇩

Philip Howard
(1944—)

Selected Bibliography

Alexander, John, & Lazell, James, *Ribbon of Sand, the Amazing Convergence of the Ocean & the Outer Banks*, Chapel Hill & London, The University of North Carolina Press, 1992

Ballance, Alton, *Ocracokers*, Chapel Hill & London, The University of North Carolina Press, 1989

Carbone, John S., *The Civil War in Coastal North Carolina*, Raleigh, North Carolina Department of Cultural Resources, Division of Archives and History, 2001

Cecelski, David, *The Waterman's Song, Slavery and Freedom in Maritime North Carolina*, Chapel Hill & London, The University of North Carolina Press, 2000

Cloud, Ellen Fulcher, *Ocracoke Lighthouse*, Spartanburg, SC, The Reprint Company, 1993

Duffus, Kevin, *The Last Days of Black Beard the Pirate*, Raleigh, Looking Glass Productions, 2008

Lee, Robert E., *Blackbeard the Pirate, A Reappraisal of His Life and Times*, Winston-Salem, John F. Blair, 1974

Mobley, Joe A., *Ship Ashore! The U.S. Lifesavers of Coastal North Carolina*, Raleigh, North Carolina Department of Cultural Resources, Division of Archives and History, 1994

O'Neal, Calvin; Rondthaler, Alice; & Fletcher, Anita, editors, *The Story of Ocracoke Island*, Swan Quarter, NC, Hyde County Historical Society, 1976

O'Neal, Earl, *Howards, Garrishes, Jacksons & Stowes of Ocracoke Island, North Carolina, Their Ancestors and Descendants*, Ocracoke, Earl W. O'Neal, Jr., 2007

Padgett, Dora Adelle, *William Howard Last Colonial Owner of Ocracoke Island, North Carolina, His Family and Descendants*, Washington, D.C., Port City Press, Inc., 1974

Payne, Roger L., *Place Names of the Outer Banks*, Washington, NC, Thomas A. Williams, 1985

Stick, David, *Graveyard of the Atlantic*, Chapel Hill, The University of North Carolina Press, 1952

Stick, David, *NC Lighthouses*, Raleigh, North Carolina Department of Cultural Resources, Division of Archives and History, 1980

Stick, David, *The Outer Banks of North Carolina, 1584-1958*, Chapel Hill, The University of North Carolina Press, 1958

Stick, David, *Roanoke Island, the Beginnings of English America*, Chapel Hill, The University of North Carolina Press, 1983

Whedbee, Charles, *Blackbeard's Cup and Stories of the Outer Banks*, Winston-Salem, John F. Blair, 1989

Whedbee, Charles, *Legends of the Outer Banks*, Winston-Salem, John F. Blair, 1966

Williamson, Sonny, *Shipwrecks of Ocracoke Island*, Marshallberg, NC, Grandma Publications, 2000

Wood, Virginia Steele, *Live Oaking, Southern Timber for Tall Ships*, Annapolis, MD, Naval Institute Press, 1981

ACKNOWLEDGMENTS

THIS book would never have been possible if it were not for the many Ocracokers who kept our stories alive generation after generation.

O'cockers, of course, told the stories (on front porches, around kitchen tables, on docks, or aboard sailing vessels) not so I could write a book. The stories were told for their children and grandchildren—to entertain, to pass on family history, to honor local heroes, and to celebrate our unique island culture…or just to pass the time on a hot summer's day while the meal wine was working.

A number of Ocracoke natives and residents deserve special mention for preserving the stories and for sharing them with me. I list them in alphabetical order: Maurice Ballance, Mildred Bryant, Muzel Bryant, Betty Helen Howard Chamberlin, Ellen Marie Fulcher Cloud, Euphemia Gaskins Ennis, Ward Garrish, Clayton Gaskill, Edgar Howard, Elizabeth O'Neal Howard, Julia Howard, Lawton Howard, Sr., Lawton Howard, Jr., Walter Howard, Jr., George Guthrie Jackson, Nathaniel Jackson, Blanche Howard Jolliff, Martha Dean Howard Kennedy, Robert Kennedy, Chester Lynn, Dale Mutro, Bertha O'Neal, Calvin O'Neal, Charlie Morris O'Neal, Chloe O'Neal, Earl O'Neal, Fowler O'Neal, John O'Neal, Lorena O'Neal, Mildred O'Neal, Elizabeth Parsons, Roy Parsons, Alton Scarborough, Blanche Styron, Mary (Dallie) Howard Turner, Myra Wahab, Larry Williams.

In addition to those mentioned above I have had invaluable assistance from the staff of the Ocracoke Preservation Society, many other Ocracoke natives and residents, and even a few visitors. I always knew I could turn to certain neighbors, friends, and relatives in order to flesh out a story with names, dates, or additional anecdotes. Without their help this book could not have been written. My heartfelt thanks goes to them all.

I am especially indebted to Jim Fineman, Julie Howard, Blanche Jolliff, Earl O'Neal, Lee Sauer, Al Scarborough, and Dallie Turner for reading my early manuscripts with diligence and a keen eye, and for their many valuable suggestions. This work is far better because of their honest comments.

Although all of the stories contained in this volume follow a long tradition of oral transmission and many have never before been put into print, some of the stories have been recorded previously. I refer the reader to the bibliography for additional island history and further reading.

This book would never have been written without the encouragement and enthusiastic support of adopted Ocracoker, Lou Ann Homan-Saylor. As Elizabeth Parsons so aptly put it, "She's one of us."

A very special word of thanks goes to Blanche Howard Jolliff, my second cousin once removed, whose prodigious memory and love of Ocracoke were invaluable in making many of these beloved stories come delightfully alive. Besides, it was always a pleasure to visit with her and chat about old times.

I offer my apologies to any islanders whose names I have omitted or who find inevitable mistakes in this collection. I have made every effort to verify facts, dates, names, and other details. In the end, all errors are entirely mine.

Photo credits

Front Cover:
Graveyard on Howard Street, Amy Howard.
Back Cover:
Evans Howard's tombstone, Philip Howard
Author's photo, Jim Fineman.
Chapter One:
Lighthouse, Philip Howard
Chapter Three:
Island Inn Stairs, Lou Ann Homan
Chapter Four:
Captain Thomas House, Lou Ann Homan
Chapter Seven:
USLSS Quarters, Amy Howard
Chapter Eight:
Lighthouse, Lou Ann Homan
Fresnel Lens, Dale Mutro
Lighthouse Stairway, Lou Ann Homan
Haunted Cottage, Lou Ann Homan
Chapter Nine:

Springer's Point, Lou Ann Homan
Clay Pipes, Amy Howard
Chapter Eleven:
Lighthouse & McWilliams House, Lou Ann Homan
Chapter Fifteen:
Cemetery, Amy Howard

All of the other photos are provided courtesy of Earl O'Neal, Jr. who has made an extensive collection of vintage Ocracoke Island photos gathered from a number of island residents and the Ocracoke Preservation Society.